Never Anything Too Easy

Never Anything Too Easy

N.A.T.E.

An Autobiography by
Nathaniel J. Henry

NeverAnythingToo Easy.com

NNSJA Publishing, Inc.
CHICAGO, ILLINOIS

First printing 2000
Second printing 2008

ISBN 10: 0-9670584-5-7
ISBN 13: 978-0-9670584-5-0
LCCN: 99-96044

ATTENTION CORPORATIONS, UNIVERSITIES, COLLEGES, AND PROFESSIONAL ORGANIZATIONS: Quantity discounts are available on bulk purchases of this book for educational purposes. Special books or book excerpts can also be created to fit specific needs. For information, please contact:
NNSJA Publishing, Inc., 6238 North Hoyne, Ste 3D, Chicago, IL 60659
phone 773-852-9504; email NateHenry78@hotmail.com

**Visit us on the World Wide Web @
www.NeverAnythingTooEasy.com**

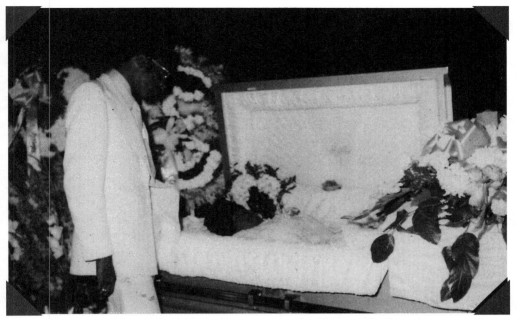

My father, Nathaniel Sr., looking over my mother, Theresa, at her funeral.

I would like to dedicate this book to Mrs. Theresa Henry, my mother, who passed away before I had a chance to know her. To all foster and DCFS children in the world, I give you this actuation tool as you reach for the unthinkable. On behalf of parents who have had their children taken away by the courts, stay strong; I feel your pain!

—Nathaniel J. Henry

ACKNOWLEDGMENTS

To my wonderful children, Nathaniel III, Nicosia, Shaquille, Jocqui, and Ashanti Henry, who will always be the love of my life. You have been the motivating force that has helped me to complete this astonishing book. Daddy never meant to cause you any pain. I will always love all of you no matter what obstacles stand in my way. I would like to express my deepest gratitude to my father, Nathaniel Senior, my two sisters Niece and Lenette, and my brother Keefe. You are all very special to me; when Mama died you stayed strong and continued supporting me when no one else did and gave me strength to continue on in life.

To William Berry, Bobby Jackson, Carl Davis, John Stewert, M. Kelly, Johnny Westmoreland, and Rap Artist Rhyme for listening when I needed someone to talk to. To Keith Kreiter, my agent, whom I look at as a part of the family, for giving me the chance to prove myself in this world of nonbelievers. Nicole Berngard, you are a very special person who came along and rescued me from the curve of death. You believed I could reach higher levels and deserved the very best out of life. Thanks to Lisa E. and Barbara Gaino from WGCI radio for enhancing my project. A new addition to my life, the powerful motivational speaker Les Brown, has helped make me a diamond. All of my rough edges have been smoothed out and I no longer worry about things I can't control. Les told me, "If you can look up, then you can get up." This is how I stayed inspired throughout my journey. Special thanks to everyone else who has been there for me through the ups and downs of my Never-Anything-Too-Easy life.

SPECIAL THANKS

Special thanks goes out to: L.A. Lyte Studios, Inc.; Marilyn and Tom Ross, Sue Collier, Cathy Bowman, Kate Deubert and everyone else at About Books, Inc. I would also like to thank Shelley Sapyta, Scott Denman and colleagues at BookMasters; Robin Bright at Baker & Taylor; Margaret Anne Slawson and everyone at Access Publishers Network; Beverly Humphries for efficiently and responsibly taking me under her wing, as well as the rest of my colleagues at Lydia Children's Home; Gerald Washington, Ava George and CYC Lower North Center colleagues; Jacqueline Johnson and colleagues at Thresholds Bridge West psychiatric rehabilitation centers..

My sisters Lisa, Natalie and Little Linda; my brothers Eric and Jeffrey George; Mrs. Jackson; Brian Burns; Molly and Ivan Burns; Mr. and Mrs. Lula Walker and family; and all of my nieces and nephews.

My professor, Dr. Harold Hild, from Northeastern Illinois University; Mrs. Betty Field from Northeastern Illinois University; Dr. Renee Jones from Triton College; Pete Babcock from the NBA Atlanta Hawks; Chicago singer/song writer R. Kelly; Pro Am Basketball Tournament announcers Smitty and Snake; Hoop Dreams movie stars Arthur Agee and William Gates; and Chicago song writer/producer M.Doc; Wild Style; and, Crucial Conflict.

Another special thanks goes out to Dan Roan from Channel 9 News; Harry Porterfield from Channel 7 News in Chicago; Gary

Reinmouth, Chicago Tribune; Quention Curtis from Salon Sense magazine; and Willie Scott from Scott's Design.

Former foster child and now DCFS administrator Rico Echevarria, and his brother, my partner in crime, middle light-weight boxer from Chicago Israel Echevarria—through our hard times in DCFS, thanks. Also to Chi's funniest comedian for the next millennium, Corey Hit Man Holcomb, and to my friend, Chicago heavy-weight boxer representing the U.S. in the 2000 Olympics, Michael Bennett. I also want to thank NFL's Chris Penn and Chicago Bulls' Randy Brown. A special shout goes out to all the "Ballers" that are putting it down in Chi Town; Chris Brown, his son NBA Shannon Brown and family; Larry Parker, his daughter WNBA Candace Parker, and son NBA Anthony Parker; best girls basketball coaches in the world—Bolingbrook High School's Tony Smith and assistant Sgt. Larry; No Book No Ball president Brian McKinney; Sanctuary; Entertainment Lawyer Dale Golden; CEO of Joe Rizza Ford, Dan McMillan; and best principal, Bolingbrook High School's James Mitchum.

Special thanks to the mothers of my beautiful children, Nicosia, Krystal, and grandmother Inez, grandfather Claude, consins R & B sensations Cherish and their grandmother Aunt Geraldine and family, Illinois State championship basketball tournament announcer Lee Hall, my twin brother Khalil and Abnar Farrkham, my close friend, our future president Barack Obama, his wife Michelle, her brother head mens basketball coach Craig Robinson, and special thanks go out to Megan and her mother Nancy, for without you all, a lot of this would not have been possible, my guy Chris Gissendanner and family, Dorian Welch, my buddy Sherron Collins from NCAA champions Kansas University Jayhawks, Reggie and lil' brother Simeon High School phenomenon NBA Derrick Rose. Thank you to long-time friend Ronnie Lester, NBA L.A. Lakers, and Chicago's very own legendary NBA Sunny Parker.

Last, but not least, all of the kids at CYC's Lower North Center in Cabrini Greens; the foster kids at Lydia Children's Home, Lawrence Hall, Maryville Academy, and all children in foster care agencies across America.

Keep in mind I'm no different from you!

Love - N.A.T.E.

CONTENTS

PREFACE

I, Nathaniel Jocquis Henry, did not appear to have much chance of success in life. Being born in 1970 and raised in Chicago by a rather poor family, I was not given proper structure. People need to realize that in a city—regardless of its size—a person can go through many unavoidable struggles. I was educated at Northeastern Illinois University and graduated with degrees in Psychology and Communications. I am currently pursuing a Master's Degree in Speech.

Because of my love for children, they have inspired me to keep writing this book. There were many times I cried, had migraine headaches, and suffered from mental fatigue. Looking deep into my past and focusing on the adversity I've overcome, it was distressing to acquaint the world with these emotions. Knowing that I have accomplished the impossible, I am dedicated to sharing my belief that regardless of one's socioeconomic background, dreams do come true!

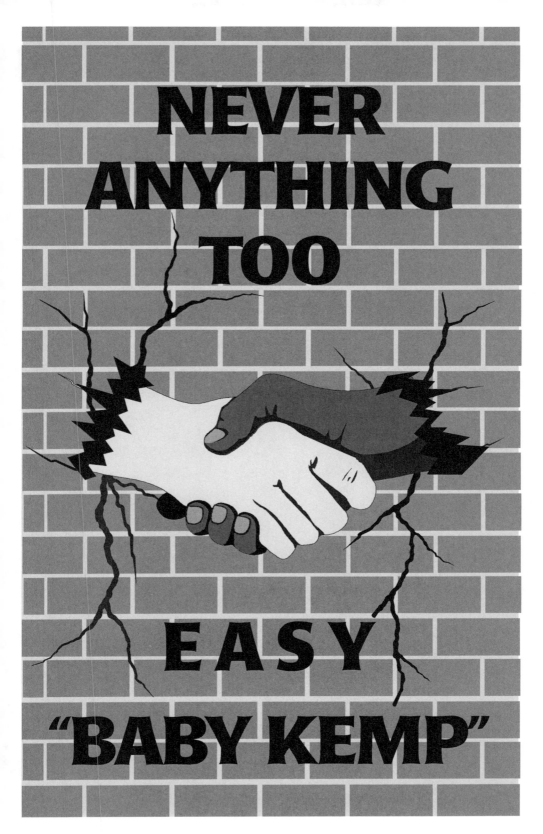

CHAPTER 1

Family Separation

It all started when my mother died of a terrible disease called encephalitis when I was five years old. I could remember my father asking me, "Son, will you take care of me?" I replied, "Yes." I do not blame my father for giving up his kids, because he lost a significant other and he could no longer take care of his children. Mentally, it was ripping him up inside. When the pain became too much, my sisters, brother, and I went to live with my maternal grandmother.

Me, Nathaniel Henry, Jr. at the tender age of five.

My father meant for this to be a temporary arrangement and thought he would get his children back when he got over the pain. My grandparents, however, refused to give up custody. My father begged and asked them, "Why are you doing this? These are my children." They replied, "These are my daughter's kids and we will be taking care of them from now on." My father did not know what to do. He thought that by letting my grandparents keep us while recovering from the loss of his wife, he was

(From top to bottom) My older sister Untrea, my younger sister Lerhashnia, and my younger brother Keefe.

actually taking care of us. My grandparents believed they were best fit to take care of me and my siblings.

Daddy shed many tears as he fought for custody in the court system, but he lost the battle. Niece (Untrea), Lenette (Lerhashnia), Keefe, and I were finally split up. My two sisters went to live with our aunt and Keefe went to live with our grandmother. I was made a ward of the court because I fought too much in school. My grandparents claimed they could not handle me, but it was just that my name was Nate. I was named after my father Nathaniel Henry Senior. My grandparents hated him so much they told me I was just like him. They would compare me to my father and say I was going to end up in jail. Whatever their reasons, I was awarded to the state without a father, mother, brother, or sisters.

In order to understand the ramifications of my situation, let me define the Department of Children and Family Services. DCFS is a service that deals with the licensing of daycare centers, homes, and foster care providers. The majority of its services are for children who are wards of the state. Being a ward of the state means the child is in the custody of the state and it is the state's responsibility to care for that child until he or she is legally independent. The DCFS places children who are in the custody of the state into foster homes. Most children are placed in temporary foster homes and they are moved on a regular basis. The children will move an average of three to six times in the system when they are placed in temporary homes.

DCFS also provides services for children who are not wards of the state and are still living with their parents. Services are given to what they call intact families. Intact families are part of the DCFS system because of abuse or neglect of children. The intact families receive counseling, homemaker services, daycare benefits, and sometimes financial assistance.

The intention of the system is to save children, but the DCFS hinders more than helps. The DCFS system does not provide a stable environment. A child needs security; moving from home to home does not establish a sense of equilibrium. Providing a child with shelter, food, and clothing is not enough for proper development. Children need to know they are loved and wanted; this feeling of wholeness is the key element to becoming a success. The DCFS system provides children with the bare necessities, but it does not provide children with love and developmental skills, both of which are extremely important to a child's development.

Children have more needs than the DCFS services provide. The DCFS system cannot ensure that every child it places will have the emotional support and attention necessary to develop the proper mentality about themselves throughout life. I know the system cannot do everything needed to help children, but it can give more support through mentor and role model programs. These are likely to help many children feel more positive about themselves. Children who feel noble about themselves know that God always cares for them. Anyone can conquer their hopes and dreams if they just believe they can do "all things through Christ that strengthens them." We can all achieve our dreams if we just keep the faith!

During the time I was in the DCFS, I was lonely many nights. Sometimes I didn't think I would make it—and I was only five years old. I was in groups with gang bangers, murderers, and drug dealers. I was terrified. The minute we got out of hand the staff would give us shots of Thorazine to slow us down.

My form of release was fighting. I missed my mother so much and could not understand why she left me, so I went on a rampage in the group homes. The staff would give me a shot every day and lock me in a room for punishment. I would cry, thinking about my brother and sisters and wondering why my father hadn't come to get me out of here.

My father had not given up on me. He fought the system for years and was finally awarded custody of me under one condition: I had to move in with my other grandmother—my father's mother—and visit a therapist twice a week. My father agreed readily, saying, "Yes, whatever, I just want my boy out of here!"

Nathaniel Henry, Sr., my father.

I was twelve years old and still living with my grandmother and her kids. I was not allowed to live with my father because the court decided he was not stable enough financially to take care of me. He visited me twice a week and we would have fun. But then he would leave and I would start crying.

When my grandmother went to church, she would take her two daughters and leave me home with her oldest son, Donald, who was 31. I didn't know he was gay until he made sexual advances toward me. It went on for a couple of months and he said he would hurt me "really bad" if I told anyone. I wanted to tell my father what was happening to me, but I feared for my life. I was afraid of what my father would do to Donald if he found out what was happening. I didn't want my father to go to jail.

I kept quiet until Donald tried to perform oral sex on me.

He told me to take all of my clothes off. I undressed but left on only my underwear. He came into the room and threatened to beat me if I didn't take them off by the time he counted to ten. When he got to two, I picked up the iron from off the floor and swung it so hard at his face it knocked him out. I put on my clothes and ran all the way to the police station three miles away. He was picked up that same night but they did not hold him.

The police asked my grandmother what happened; she lied to them, saying I started the fight. She said her son was not gay and they believed her story. I was placed right back in DCFS. So there I was, almost thirteen and I hadn't seen my sisters or brother for years. I didn't even know if they were still alive. I tried to maintain and stay focused but I missed my family. This separation was killing me inside.

In 1982 I was placed in Herrick House, a group home located in Bartlett, Illinois. I lived there a year before I was moved again. While at Herrick House I worked a summer job on campus grounds. This enabled me to get away from the dorms during the day and I was able to save a little money. Another benefit was that residents who had jobs were looked at differently among the staff. They were respected more and given special privileges like being able to leave campus. This special indulgence was rare because normally residents were not allowed to leave the grounds.

To take my mind off the pain I felt from being separated from my family, the residents tried to talk to me and play games. I had no desire to participate so I would ignore them. This caused the staff to take my "points" away; the more points they took away the fewer privileges I received. It got to the point where I started fighting with the residents and even some of the staff. They tried to give me more Thorazine, but it didn't help. Finally, they resorted to calling the police, who restrained me and escorted me away in handcuffs. The staff had decided to force me out of the group home.

CHAPTER 2

Experiencing Turbulence

In their report the staff declared me mentally disturbed and transferred me to Reed Mental Health Center, a locked facility. At the time, I knew there was nothing wrong with me. I was surrounded by a group of unbalanced fools! Yet, regardless of how much I hated it there, I had to stay six months for a behavioral evaluation. Doctors diagnosed me with a brain-based neuro-behavioral disorder, to which they attributed my behavioral problems. The analysis was then made that I was capable of controlling my actions and avoiding trouble. I was soon released from that ward and transferred to a subdivision of that institution across the street, also a locked facility. I was relieved to be out of the mental ward, even though I was still a part of the Reed Mental Health Center.

There were strict rules—no going outside, no visitors. I remember a bully who always picked on everybody. One day he came over to my table during lunch and demanded I give him my meal. When I refused, he took the food and then pushed my head back with his hand. I felt as if my head was no longer connected to my body. The bully went back to his table and acted as if nothing had happened. I became so angry, I picked up a chair and broke it across his neck. There was blood everywhere. He fell on the dining room floor with his face flat in a pool of blood for 50 minutes. I thought I killed him!

After that incident, I could have gone to jail or been kicked out of the placement home. Because I was only 13, I was put in an "audyhome," a correctional center for young teens. It was a locked facility with only a glass window to keep you in touch with reality. While at the audyhome I was able to do a lot of thinking because I was locked in a room 22 hours a day. The only time I was let out of my room was to shower, eat, watch a little TV, and talk to the staff.

My father visited when he could. He tried to encourage me, saying, "Son, stay strong! You are a winner! You are going to get out of here." He brought me things to read, which helped keep my mind strong and focused. I read the Bible, books, magazines—you name it, I read it. This helped make the time go faster and had the added benefits of educating me and increasing my vocabulary.

As I got to know the staff, they always told me, "Nate, you have good sense. You don't need to be here." I would use big words I learned from books in order to impress the staff. They would ask me what the word meant. I replied, "Look it up in your dictionary." I would never let on I didn't even know what the word meant. This was the only way I could have the ups on them!

From that point on I knew I had an effect on them. When the day came for me to be discharged, I had behaved so well and impressed them so much they had no choice but to dismiss me. I was relocated to a place called McCormick House. During the seven-and-a-half-hour drive I looked out of the window wondering where I was going now. I was scared as hell. I considered jumping out of the truck, but we were moving so fast I figured it would be just my luck to jump out, survive and be left in critical condition for the rest of my life. This was to be my fourth placement in the DCFS system, but little did I know how much it would build my character and give me a chance to show off my athletic abilities. Being able to see that I was good at something gave me the strength to go on.

To feel more at home I got to know the other boys in the group home as well as the staff members. There was one kid who didn't like me. His name was Charles and he was from the Robert Taylor Projects in Chicago. Every day when we had our group meetings, Charles would try to say things to provoke me. He would tell the staff, "Nate left the bathroom dirty," "Nate plays his music too loud," "Nate went into the kitchen and made some food without permission." For that reason, I would lose my privileges and be dropped to a lower level. The level system was used for disciplining us at the group home when we didn't follow routines or misbehaved.

I got fed up with Charles and the sneaky things he did. For example, I would go to school and when I returned all of my clothes were gone. I knew who had them. The very next day Charles would be wearing my clothes. I would say, "Hey, Charles, that's my shirt." He would reply, "You better get the fuck out of my face. I just bought this yesterday." I let it go and the very next day he would repeat the same scenario over again. I confronted him again and instead of him answering me back he stole on me. (This is when one person hits or swings in the face of another person.) I swear I must have beaten his ass as if I were crazy. I thought about all those days he lied and got me in trouble. Being new to Mc Cormick House, I had; no support and therefore could not do anything about it. Coming to McCormick House out of the audyhome, I already had a bad record and wanted to avoid being sent back.

Once again Charles provoked me, and I couldn't hold it in any longer. I slammed him on the ground and beat him until he couldn't move. When I stopped 20 minutes later I walked down the stairs and heard somebody yell, "I'm going to kill you!" I turned just in time to see Charles swing at my head with a baseball bat. He missed but caught my elbow and broke it in three places. If I had not ducked in time, I would not be here to tell you this story. I ran outside to try and get away but he followed me. One of the staff noticed what was going on and ran behind Charles. The staff eventually caught up with him and made him put the bat down, then he called the police. I knew they were going to take me again, but they took Charles instead. I was relieved but my arm was in a cast the whole summer.

By fall 1983 my elbow had heeled just in time for my new beginning as a freshman at Kenwood Academy High School. At McCormick House we were able to attend public schools, which was new for me. Little did I know this was about to change my whole life. For once in my life I could see promise, hope, and a successful future.

CHAPTER 3

Does Happiness Last?

As the semester continued, I made a smooth transition in adjusting to the outside world. I had never before interacted with so many kids of different ethnic backgrounds. Since the school was located in upscale Hyde Park, the majority of the students were rich, although there were middle class and poor kids as well. I felt lucky to be at Kenwood and planned to take advantage of this opportunity.

I walked through the halls, my mind wandering and thinking about all the bad times in my life. The thoughts were so deep that I missed my first period class one day and fell down the stairs. The students in the hallways laughed hard, but I wasn't hurt—some would say I had now been initiated as a freshman. And to me, all the jokes in the world at my expense couldn't keep me from feeling free from the hell I had been through up to this point.

Even the rhythm and blues king R. Kelly, with whom I actually attended school, was poor and considered a bum. Although "Rob" was a junior and I a freshman, all the so-called bums hung out together after school.

I remember when Kenwood held tryouts for the track team. There were several hundred kids trying out, and it was the last

11

day to go out for the team. The first heat (group of runners) was asked to line up, including me. I had never run track before, but I knew I was fast because I used to always run from the police and gang bangers.

We were getting ready to run the 400 meter, which is once around the track. There were just two freshman, me and another kid; the rest of the runners were sophomores, juniors, and seniors. The gunman said to the crowd that was watching—including R. Kelly—to move off the track. There were about 2,500 people, so it took 10 to 15 minutes to get them cleared. The gunman told the runners to take their mark.

As the race was about to start I began to collect my thoughts. To motivate myself, I tried to imagine I was being chased again. When the gunman signaled, I dashed out of the blocks at full speed, flying around the curves of the track like a cheetah. I was moving so fast, it was as if my feet were not touching the ground. Everyone else was way behind me. When I went over the finish line, I said to the coach, "I told you I wouldn't let you down!" The next thing I knew, everyone was congratulating me because I had just broken a record.

The state record for the 400 meter for all of the high schools was 50 seconds. The world record at the time was 45 seconds and I ran it in 46 seconds. Overnight, I became a sensation. Everyone at school suddenly knew my name. Girls in the hallway whispered things like, "That's him. He's cute." The senior guys wanted me to hang out with them, smoking pot and cigarettes. Instead, I found my own crowd to hang out with.

If I caved in to peer pressure, I could lose everything I had gained. The kids at Kenwood had no idea I was a kid from the DCFS. I was just a freshman, but growing up in the system had pushed me to grow up fast. Kids in the system were not supposed to be with those in the mainstream world. It was almost as if the state wanted these children to believe they could not compete academically, verbally, or athletically with others. I had shown them they were wrong. Winning the race was my way of showing myself and the state that DCFS kids could compete with the outside world. If I screwed up I would have been right back where I started. This was the beginning of a new life for me. A freshman with a lot of recognition and respect was how I was perceived in other people's eyes.

Classes at Kenwood often included seniors, juniors, sophomores, and freshman in the same classes. R. Kelly and I were in the same music class, taught by Miss McLean. Before he became famous we hung out together, because all the bums stuck together. Rob always encouraged me, telling me I was going to go pro because I was just a freshman and already the fastest kid in school. I appreciated his encouragement and wondered if maybe he was right and this could be my ticket out of the DCFS system.

Whenever Rob had his keyboard with him, he stopped in the hallways to sing. The hall officers hated to break up the crowd that gathered but, of course, that was their duty. Rob sounded so much like Stevie Wonder, everyone was amazed. Still, because he was considered a bum at the school, he was nobody special there. He was a great person in my life. R. Kelly helped give me a sense of direction while I was at Kenwood.

The state allowed me to stay at a public school as long as I kept up my grades. I maintained a 3.4 grade point average while running track and living in a group home. The authorities were startled by my success in school and constantly tried to insinuate my extracurricular activities were interfering with my scholastics and house chores. But I knew I could do it and had no plans to mess up. Mr. Key, my track coach, was especially happy when the group home gave me permission to stay on the team. He had high hopes for me and said I could be one of the top track runners in the nation.

The state actually had a hidden agenda—they didn't want one child to excel more than the other children. They thought it would cause a conflict in the household. This way, our minds would develop based on the system's reality. Many had already come to the conclusion I had too many privileges and going to an outside school for me was enough. Rather than be happy for me, that I was able to assimilate to the mainstream world and be successful, I feel they really wanted me to fail.

There are many staff members and group home directors who preach how they want their children to be successful. In fact, they are not concerned with the welfare of the child. To the outside world, it looks as if they are devoted to helping disadvantaged children. The truth of the matter was that once you turned 18, you were no longer their responsibility. If you were to go to jail or be locked up as a result of your negative behavior, they would disown you. Their sole purpose was to come into work, not perform their duties, and get paid.

The system wanted you to utilize what you could while you were there, but the problem was they would provoke you into messing up so that they could take your points or drop you down a level. Thinking about taking advantage of the things that were being offered to you was not even a conscious thought, because you were busy just trying to maintain level-headiness every day while you were there.

In 1984, I had a class called consumer education. The teacher found out I was a ward of the state and made no effort to conceal his resentment. He asked me things like, "What are you doing in this school?" He told me about another student he had who hadn't done well in the class because he had lived in a bad boys home.

He told me daily I should drop the course. In class he embarrassed me by asking, "Nate, what do you think it would take to get out of the system, since you are in foster care?" The whole class looked at me in shock. I felt like running out of the class. I was hurt and speechless. It took me several minutes to answer the question. With a tear rolling down my cheek, I said, "That question has nothing to do with consumer education." After class was dismissed he came over to me and said, "When I ask you a question boy . . . answer it and don't get smart about it."

My first reaction was to knock his ass out! But I knew I would have gone to jail and that's just what he wanted me to do. I kept my composure and walked out of the classroom. He called me, but I kept on walking. The next day he wasn't going to let me back in the classroom so I went straight to the principal and told her what happened.

The principal set up a meeting with the teacher, me, and a group home staff member. I was told to leave the office so I didn't know what was said; from that point on I was not called for any more after-class meetings. I was able to do the course work, but the teacher still didn't let up on me. I was doing A and B work and he still wouldn't give me the grade I deserved. Going to class was already difficult, passing through the hallways where students were whispering about me being a ward of the state and giving me funny looks.

I felt like dropping out. The entire school knew my situation, but I stayed strong and kept coming to school every day. I managed to pass consumer education with a C. I marked this down as another victory for the kids in foster care systems.

Never Anything Too Easy is the name of this book—and spells out my name N-A-T-E— for a reason. Everything in my life has always been difficult. If there was an obstacle in my way, I was left with a decision to make. I could choose to let it stop me and bring me down, or choose to go around it. I knew God didn't bring me this far to leave me.

When my mother was alive we went to church almost every day. I think this has been a strong force in my life. I remember a song the choir used to sing that goes a little something like this: "Nobody told me that the road would be easy; I don't believe He brought me this far to leave me." I always thought about that song when things didn't go right, when it seemed like everywhere I went people put me down.

My sophomore year at Kenwood was a hard one. I worked two jobs, one at a fast food restaurant after 4:00 PM on weekdays, and another job on the weekends from 1:00 until 9:30 PM. I worked two jobs so I wouldn't have to be at the group home very often. The other boys there were always hassling me and trying to get me into trouble. It was a stressful situation for me and I began to wonder if it was all worth it.

During all of this work, I was a young guy just 14 years old and I was going through all this shit! I couldn't lose it. If I did, the staff members would have sent me back to lock-up. I didn't know what to do, it seemed like life wasn't as precious to me anymore. I didn't feel like I had a cause, I would get on my knees and pray to God every day, sometimes two hours a day. I had to be strong. I kept telling myself this, "After I have done all I can, I put it in the Lord's hands and let him work it out." Somehow the pain started going away gradually and the house had cooled down for a while.

I was just 14 years old and the jobs started to take a lot out of me. I wasn't eating right and my grades were slipping a bit, which was the last thing I needed. If it had gotten back to the staff at the group home, they would have surely made me quit my jobs. But I needed the jobs not only to avoid being at the group home but to save money. As track season rolled around I had to make a decision: Should I keep the jobs or run track? I knew I had to at least keep one job or I would have no money at all and I'd be a bum all over again.

I decided to quit the fast food restaurant, which really didn't pay very well anyway. As track season approached, I was looking forward to an excellent year. I wasn't about to let anybody down, especially myself.

Then the news came. I had to leave Kenwood Academy High School. I couldn't believe it was happening, after I had tried so hard. I had letters from so many universities, I was sure I would get a scholarship. I thought I could even make the Olympics. (Imagine those headlines: "Ward of State Goes to Olympics"!)

My coach had delivered the bad news to me while we were practicing. With tears streaming down his face, he told me I was no longer a part of the track team. McCormick House had ordered my transfer to another group home. Although the coach had begged them to let me stay and even offered to let me live with him, they refused to reconsider.

I didn't know where I was going to be placed or why. Just when I was gaining acceptance at Kenwood and feeling good about myself, they relocated me for seemingly no reason. The staff didn't even try to fight for me, and they weren't concerned about my success. They were simply following the rules, however senseless they were. This is why I believe the DCFS system is a scam, interested in money and not the welfare of many children. Do you still believe happiness lasts forever?

CHAPTER 4

Hopeless Tomorrows

I remember cleaning out my locker and the kids would walk by and ask, "Is it true you are leaving?" Yes, I would say, and some of my friends started crying. It was such a dispirited day for me, the time seemed to go so slowly. Where was I going? Would it be another locked placement?

I went back to McCormick House to grab my things; they wanted me out of there the same day. The staff seemed happy to be getting rid of me. I couldn't understand it; in no way had I disrespected them to the point where I should be taken out of school and kicked out of the group home. They ruined my chances for a track scholarship. If there ever was a time I was broke down, it was that day. I was deeply hurt and could not see why they seemed to have it in for me. They were supposed to care for kids.

This was truly a tough moment in my life, but I didn't give up on having faith that God would see me through. At 15, I was placed in Lawrence Hall Youth Services. I went two months without talking to anyone. I still couldn't believe I wasn't at Kenwood Academy. I couldn't even begin to compare and contrast Kenwood to Lawrence Hall. Their schools were right on campus with the group homes. I cried every day I was in this place. Until one day a staff member talked to me; her name was Tina.

She tried to encourage me. "Nate," she said, "coming from a fine school like Kenwood Academy, it is going to be a difficult adjustment. At Lawrence Hall we try to provide you with the same opportunities as you had before. Nate, you don't have to stop working hard because you're in a reform school. The same activities you were doing at Kenwood, whether it's running track or getting good grades, you can do it here. Nobody can keep you down, but you're going to have to work harder to be able to go to college. You can still go pro in track and become anything you want to if you put your mind and heart into it."

When I received her advice, I changed. I was suddenly able to go to school and interact with the students and faculty. It seemed as though God sent my mother down from the heavens through Tina. I had never gotten a positive message from any of the staff members all the while I was in the state system. I felt secure with Tina because she cared about the kids who came through Lawrence Hall.

Gradually, I opened up a little every day although I was still sad. I would come home from school and go right to my room; staff would ask me what was wrong and I would snap at them. They retaliated by taking points from our daily behavior sheets.

Lawrence Hall was run by a point system ranging from level one being the lowest to level four being the highest. If you were on level four, you could go anywhere. But it was difficult to get to level four because of the staff. They weren't all like Tina. They regularly held a staffing, which is when all the staff met to discuss the behavior of the children there. If any child endangered or cursed at a staff member, he or she was dropped to the lowest possible level. At one staffing, my behavior was discussed. I was assigned to a therapist to talk to daily about what made me snap the way I did.

Lawrence Hall had read my file from the previous institution, so every time I went off it was written down. The therapist was aware of it before I got to her office. The first question out of her mouth was, "Nate, why do you keep repeating this negative behavior at every placement?" I explained how much I missed my family and, every time I thought about them and how I couldn't get to them, I became angry. She said this behavior was understandable but cursing out staff was not the correct way to release frustration. She suggested that instead of taking my anger out on the staff, I should take a deep breath and count to 10 or 15 until I was calm. I had tried this before, but the method didn't work for me.

The therapist told me if I kept up the negative behavior I would be kicked out of Lawrence Hall. I did my best to calm down, but I began to question why God would put me through all this pain. That is where I went wrong—I should never have questioned God. We always want our problems solved immediately, and if they aren't, the devil starts you to think there may not be a God. This is when you need to have faith. It might not happen when you want it to happen, it may not even happen next year, but keep the faith and God's grace will take you through.

Time went on at Lawrence Hall although it was tough for me. I eventually got to level four and was able to look for a job. I finally got a job working for Dominick's Finer Foods, a local supermarket. I was grateful for the opportunity to work and leave the group home for a few hours. The days I wasn't scheduled to work, I often called in to see if they needed help. My hours at the store started at 3:00 PM and some nights I wouldn't get off work until 2:00 in the morning! I worked so much, the manager promoted me from bagger to stock person in just three months, rather than waiting for the typical eight-month evaluation.

I wondered if I was too hard on myself, working so much. But I was willing to pay my dues to move up within the company and, if possible, become store manager some day. I always strived to be on top—whatever it was, I wanted to be the best! Living in a state institution for so long and listening to staff members talk about how far behind we were in academics, sports, and independent living skills made me want to prove them all wrong.

True, we didn't have some of the special resources they had. Financially, it was very difficult but we had our brains. If the staff or directors had given children a little positive reinforcement, there is no telling how many of those kids would have made it out of the DCFS system. There were kids I knew who could have been doctors, lawyers, engineers, or even president of the United States.

I was lucky to be self-motivated through the grace of God, because the system sure didn't provide the proper educational background. It would be hard as hell to get yourself up to do something about your current situation. Some children, even grown adults, need that push from others to keep going and to stay focused. We all need some positive feedback every once in a while. I managed to use every ounce of motivation within myself to make it each day.

Lawrence Hall taught me a lot about self-control, especially how not to go off on other people when it wasn't their fault. As much as I hated that level system, it was really effective. I worked so hard to reach level four. Sometimes the kids would provoke me so that I would feed into their negative behavior, but I wouldn't let it get to me.

I badly wanted to visit my Uncle Sunny's house for the weekend to be with someone who loved me. The visit was planned, and I was packed and ready to go. Unfortunately, I forgot to mop up the kitchen floor the previous night. The staff distributed new house chores every two weeks. Since it hadn't been two weeks yet, I didn't realize I had been assigned a different chore until I was ready to leave for my uncle's.

Mr. Williams asked me where I thought I was going. "You didn't mop the kitchen last night."

"The kitchen?" I asked. I explained that my chore was to clean the upper bathroom. He told me the schedule had been changed. When I reminded him the two-week period hadn't passed yet, he informed me there was a new rule in place. He then said without any remorse, "You'll pay more attention next time. Your home pass for this week has been denied."

With tears streaming down my face, I begged him to let me go home. I offered to do extra chores the following week. He refused! My first reaction was to leave and go AWOL, but I didn't. I gave him a hard look and went off to my room without saying another word.

The days passed, times got tougher and tougher. Still I maintained my cool and tried not to lose sight of my future. Lawrence Hall was in the process of developing an independent living program and five seniors were going to be chosen as test cases. Since I already had my own job and money saved, I was qualified to be part of the program.

The staff members knew I was ahead of the game, so I was selected as one of the first out of five to begin the program. Lawrence Hall also conducted a meeting with each one of us to explain why we had been chosen, and the fact that we would be setting standards for future kids entering the program.

CHAPTER 5

The Thrill of My Life

In spring 1988 I completed the Independent Living Program (ILP) and was now able to start looking for my own apartment. Everyone knows how happy you get when you're about to get your own place. I want you to envision how I must have been feeling at that point in my life. I felt I was finally halfway out of the system.

I was scheduled to graduate in August (because Lawrence Hall's school year was longer than the regular school schedule). After graduation, I planned to start college in September. People would tell me how I was such an incredible person and how they admired me for all I had accomplished to reach this point. I thanked them and used their praise as the motivation to keep me strong.

I had a good friend that year. Bobby Jackson lived in the community a few blocks from where I stayed. I met him at River Park. We were playing a pick-up game called 21. I was winning and he kept on trying to cheat me out of my points. A guy named Keith Ratucks, who later also became a good friend, was with him. While we were playing the game, Keith told Bobby to stop cheating. Bobby denied it and the two got into an argument. I became disgusted and told them I was quitting the game. Bobby apologized to me and we ended becoming the best of friends.

Every time I had permission from the staff to leave the grounds to play basketball, I called Bobby to come play with me. He had something I wanted badly; not only did he attend Theodore Roosevelt High School where he was a basketball star, but he had his freedom. I envied his life.

One day during that summer, my friend Bobby and I were walking back from a pick-up basketball game. On our way back to Lawrence Hall, I saw a girl reading a book. I was so shy and had been so isolated from the outside world for so long I forgot how to even talk to a girl. There was something special about this girl.

I was so nervous, I wrote a note to her. I didn't know how the words were going to come out of my mouth, and I didn't want to say the wrong thing. The note stated, "If you like me circle 'yes'; if you don't circle 'no.'" I know this was corny, but it was the only way I knew how to communicate at the time. Then I gave it to Bobby to give to her. She started to laugh and told me to come over and talk to her. Little did I know this was going to be my future wife and the mother of my five children.

The girl introduced herself as Nicosia R. Johnson. I looked into her pretty brown eyes while she was speaking to me and got goose bumps. She was so pretty and humble, it made me nervous. There was just something about her that made me want to be around her all the time.

"Nicosia," I said with a smile, "that's a beautiful name." She said, "Thank you, Nate," and the way she said my name, I knew this was the girl for me.

I was in love. Never before had I felt so good. I even told her the whole situation about me. I felt so comfortable around her. For the first time in my life I felt I belonged, for this woman reminded me of my mother so much.

That night we talked on the phone for more than two hours. It would probably have been longer if the staff hadn't made me get off the telephone. Afterward, I went to my bedroom, got on my knees, and thanked the Lord for sending such a wonderful woman into my life.

■   ■   ■

I was doing well in the Independent Living Program, working seven days a week to assure Lawrence Hall that they didn't make a mistake picking me. I wasn't making a whole lot of money at my grocery store job. I had to pay rent, lights, gas, phone, food, personal hygiene, transportation, and so forth. I had no money left for any extras. Hell, I didn't even have enough to take the el train downtown and go window shopping. But I finally made it out of the system; I just graduated and was on my way to Triton Junior College located in River Grove, Illinois.

Although Lawrence Hall gave me some extra money for the rent, I still had to take on a second job to make ends meet. On weekends I played the drums for a storefront church. I wasn't a great drum player, but I wasn't bad either. I was raised in the church and we always stayed after the service when the adults got into a deep spiritual conversation. I used to get on the drums and sometimes the preacher's son gave me lessons.

I enrolled at Triton College full-time. I tried to make the college thing work but it was difficult because I was working so much. I started going to college part-time, but it was still hard to manage. My grades started slipping and because I was receiving financial aid, I couldn't let my grade point average go below 2.0, as was the policy. I finally withdrew from all my classes. I knew I wanted to go to college but had to put that dream off until I was more stable and committed.

Once again the days grew long and tiresome, and I started to feel like a robot. One day when I was waiting at the public aid office to get food stamps, I was offered a job at Sears department store. It paid $8.45 an hour, which was much better than my other jobs.

I still kept my Dominick's job, working from 9:00 AM to 5:00 PM, then I slept for five hours before I had to be at Sears at midnight. I did this six days a week. One shift at Sears, about 2:30 in the morning, I started to get very tired. I snuck into the back room and made myself a pallet out of cardboard boxes. My plan was to sleep for a couple of hours. All the crew heads were on break and I figured I could go unnoticed for a couple of hours.

I ended up sleeping until it was time to get off work, which was 7:00 AM. The boss found me and fired me on the spot. That was the most expensive sleep I ever had in my life. Had I known I would have been fired, I would have slept for another ten hours.

I can laugh about it now, but at the time it happened it wasn't so funny. But once again I was lucky and found another job. This time, I worked as a garbage man (or a residential collector, as some would say). This had to be the hardest job I ever had. Although the company insured each man who drove a truck, they didn't want to be liable for any accidents. If you had an accident without at least 10 years of seniority, your ass was fired. You can imagine how careful I was because I couldn't afford to be fired again—I was already two months behind in my rent.

Meeting the requirements for this job wasn't a cakewalk. I needed to have a class C driver's license to operate the truck. Since I was good friends with the manager in the trucking department at Sears, I asked him if he would train me. He didn't realize I had been fired. I told him I had inherited a standard transmission vehicle from my grandfather and needed to learn how to drive it. We practiced every Saturday for two hours.

I only had a month to learn to drive a truck or the position would have been filled by someone else. With so much riding on me getting this license—such as rent, food, and bills—I *had* to pass the test. The day came for me to take the test and I was more than prepared. I had studied all night for the written test as well as training on the road and felt as ready as ready could be. Moreover this was the last day for me to show that I had attained my C class drivers license for Browning-Ferris Industries Company, better known as BFI.

I passed the written portion of the test, and then it was time to show how well I could handle a stick shift. The driving instructor had me first take the side streets. I did pretty well breaking the gears down, making sure I hit the clutch before I changed the gears. Then he had me go onto the expressway, and I was scared as hell. I couldn't tell the instructor I didn't know how to drive on the expressway for fear he wouldn't give me my license. I started praying. Funny, isn't it, how we always call on God when we want something or we're in trouble?

We proceeded onto the expressway and gradually I started changing gears to pick up speed. He told me to get off at the second exit, which I didn't really understand. It hadn't registered about the exit because I was still trying to concentrate on hitting the clutch at the right time. I took a gamble and got off at what I thought he meant; luckily, I guessed right. He told me to pull over and back up into an alley. When he told me to head back to the driving school, I was a nervous wreck because he was doing so much writing and didn't give me a clue as to if I passed or not. We pulled in and he told me I had done well and passed.

I jumped out of that truck, fell to my knees, and thanked the Lord. Then I rushed over to BFI to show them my class C license. They gave me my schedule and how much I was going to be paid: $13.95 an hour. I was so happy, for again I've beaten the odds and came up on a good-paying job. Little did I know the worst was yet to come.

The physical labor of this job was difficult. Monday through Friday, I got up at 4:00 AM to go to work. I didn't have a source of transportation and the bus out of Maywood didn't run until 6:00 AM and I had to report for work at 5:30. I had to walk 5 miles there and 5 miles back every day. Once at work, I received my route for the day. On the list there were 40 pickups on each block. There were ten blocks and one man per truck for each route.

Close your eyes and envision a big garbage truck with only one man driving and operating the truck. Each time the truck stops this man jumps out, picks up the garbage, works the hydraulic blade that holds the garbage, stops it, hops back in the truck, and pulls up to the next pile of garbage, stops, gets out, and repeats the same duty. Until one stop, I forgot to put the gears back in neutral and the truck kept rolling and almost hit a house. Even after that close encounter I had to hurry up, get myself together mentally, and help others finish their routes.

The physical labor was so hard, people were injured on a daily basis. It made others quit and the only thing that kept people there was the money, which was personally helping me pay my past due bills. I was so tired and sore from working during the week that I didn't have enough energy to go anywhere when the weekends came. I had no social life, but the situation was soon to change in the summer of 1991.

My good friend William Berry, with whom I grew up, played basketball for Triton College. He had just finished the necessary credits for an associate degree and was on his way to Ball State University on a full-ride scholarship. William, and his basketball coach from Triton, Frank Lillino, and I were sitting in front of William's house talking about what a great season he just had at Triton College. Coach Lillino asked William, who at 6 feet 9 inches was still growing, how the team would ever find a replacement for him. William told him he was standing next to a 6 foot 4 inch player with incredible speed.

Frank questioned me and I told him I had never played organized basketball before. Plus, I mentioned, I was working that garbage truck job, which had me very rusty on the basketball court. Frank said he was willing to give me a chance because of what his star player said.

By that fall I was registered for 15 credit hours. (Athletes had to have 15 or more credit hours in case they failed a course; they still would be eligible to play.) I quit my job and prepared to give this basketball thing a try.

My son Nathaniel Henry III.

Nate III imitating his daddy.

CHAPTER 6

Dreams and Illusions

I encouraged Nicosia to take 18 credit hours at school. I wanted her to hurry up and finish with junior college so she could go on to one of the big universities. If it meant that I had to quit so she could get her education first, I would oblige. I was willing to do that so she could be looked at as being a successful daughter who broke away to be with me.

I cared more about how she felt than my own feelings, and the scary part about all this was we weren't even married. I was a sucker to think she cared about me in the same way. When anger clouds your mind, people tend to forget everything they have promised. It's just like the song by Mary J. Blige: "I was a fool to let you in." Then it goes on to say, "My heart! My heart!" As you read further in the book, you will understand why I say this about Nicosia.

After Nathaniel III, Nicosia and I had two more children: a little girl named Nicosia Theresa Henry named after her mother and my mother, and Shaquille Jacques Henry named after the famous basketball star who currently plays for the Los Angeles Lakers. Shaquille's middle name came from Kansas University basketball star Jacque Vaugan, whom I met at the 1993 Nike shootout at the Rosemont Horizon.

We had three children with no family or financial support. We were about to lose our apartment because we hadn't paid rent in more than four months. Our lights and electricity were cut off. At night we would take the kids and sit in the park until the lights went out so they didn't have to sit at home in the dark. These times were full of tremendous challenges but we got through them.

In May 1993, Nicosia and I were up for graduation from Triton Junior College, and we had just received a letter in the mail that our Stafford loan checks had arrived. We were so happy because now we were able to pay our rent and bills. We speculated on whether it would be better to pay back four months of rent in Maywood or relocate to another part of Chicago. True, we had some great friends here—Michael Finley, Sherel Ford, Donny Boyce, Carl Davis, Kenny Davis, Reggie Jordan, Alonzo Verge, and others—but we had to do what was best for the family. We moved to a five-room apartment on the north side of Chicago; we had bad credit and were lucky to get approved.

Nicosia and I decided to get married. Our wedding day was May 15 at 9:00 in the morning; we graduated together that same day at 3:00 p.m. We felt it was a wise decision to get married because we had three children. We loved each other enough to know what commitment had just been made.

Nicosia went on to the University of Illinois Chicago and I chose Northeastern Illinois University across town. People often asked us why we went to separate schools, and I explained it was better for me to play basketball at NEIU rather than UIC. I always wanted to play division one basketball at a university and since I didn't play much in front of college scouts, I had to take advantage of the best opportunity. When I graduated, it was hard for me to play ball for a major division one college.

Northwestern, DePaul, and UIC were big-name schools and I knew I wasn't about to come in and play. I had a hard time getting playing time at the junior college level, so I knew noth-

38

ing was about to change at a bigger program. True, there would be a different coach, but at that level they already have a star ballplayer. I wanted a chance to play and not be used as a practice dummy.

I spoke with head coach Rees Johnson from Northeastern Illinois about playing for his basketball team. He said he had never heard of me before getting my letters. Before I left Triton I wrote Rees Johnson several times stating that I thought I could be an asset to his team. I figured I had come this far—I wasn't going to let the fact I hadn't been recruited by any colleges stop me. I had a better chance of making the team at Northeastern than anywhere else because it was a low division one program.

I tried out that whole summer going up against players such as Reggie Smith and Monte O'Quin every day. After that summer the coach made his decision to keep me on the team. I'll never forget how he said it: "Nate, congratulations. You are now a Golden Eagle." This meant so much to me because all through life I was told I wasn't going to be anything. My coach from Triton always used to say that I'd never make or play division one ball.

Nicosia and I went out that night and celebrated. We took all the kids and just enjoyed ourselves talking about how hard it was graduating from Triton College and how God blessed us. I broke down and cried for again I had beaten the odds. As Les Brown said, "No matter how hard it is or how hard it gets, I'm going to make it!"

God had blessed us by moving us into a bigger place to live and gave us two fine college institutions to attend. I had three beautiful children. I was playing basketball. I was not only happy but grateful for what God had done.

One of the greatest advantages to playing basketball at Northeastern was the traveling. I had never been anywhere outside of Chicago until then. I had never even been on an airplane before! Because I was considered a walk-on, I had to earn my place on the squad for away games to places such as California. The coaches had me play one-on-one with other players on the team to see if I was worthy to go on the trips. Rees Johnson would say, "Nate, if you win I'll take you, but if you lose I'll see you at practice when we get back." Man!

I wanted to travel so I started kicking ass. I was deadly on defense and offense. I went to California, New York, Canada, Kansas, Alabama, Wisconsin, Arizona, and Miami—places I would have probably never had the opportunity to see. I stayed at the best hotels, ate good food, met new people—all without paying a dime out of my pocket.

I remember the first time I flew. My man, Marcus West, who in 1997 played for Marquette, told me to look out the window. I almost fainted, we were so far up in the air. The city below looked like a model town with little toy figures and people who looked like ants. I was dizzy and my ears were popping. The team and coaches were having a ball laughing. Just when I thought it was over, we hit an air pocket and the plane started shaking. I thought I was going to die. It was fun, but I didn't want to play any more one-on-one for a while!

I was a walk-on who didn't receive much playing time, which was sad because I wanted to show the coaches what I could do. Some of the games seemed endless as I sat there and didn't get to play. I would sit and daydream about my family—and how I got my wife pregnant with our fourth child, Jacqui Jaleel Henry. I wondered if I should quit the team since I wasn't getting any playing time. I questioned my family's struggle to bring another baby into this world. I was really stressed out, and it seemed like nobody understood the workload I had or what it was like being Nate Henry.

My typical day usually went something like this: I awoke at 3:00 AM to get the kids up to use the bathroom so they wouldn't wet the bed. I would go back to sleep for a couple of hours, wake up my wife for school, fix the kids breakfast, drop them off at daycare, then drop off Nicosia at school. (It was a blessing we had been able to buy a small car out of our school loan money.) I would then take myself to school for the next five and a half hours. I left school by 2:30 PM to pick up Nicosia so she could have the car the second half of the day. I had to be at practice by 4:00, and she had to pick up the kids from daycare.

After practice we had to go to study hall, which was mandatory unless you were a senior or had a 3.5 GPA. If you chose not to go to study hall, you couldn't practice the next day, which meant no playing in the games. Study hall lasted two hours, so I didn't leave Northeastern until about 10:00 PM. I took the bus home because Nicosia was pregnant and the kids had to get up early in the morning, so they had to get some sleep. I often didn't get home until after midnight.

It was just too much and my body was wearing out. I didn't really want to quit, though, because that was just what people wanted me to do. "Life is going to knock you down, but when it does try to land on your back because if you can look up you can get up, land on your back" (Les Brown). God had me playing basketball for a reason and I was going to stay until I found out what it was. I needed to have something to do so I wouldn't take my frustrations out on my wife and kids.

I have met so many talented ballplayers on a personal level, many while playing in the Pro-Am Tournament with my cousin Tracy Webster, who used to hoop for the University of Wisconsin. I would like to acknowledge them at this time. With that, I'm proud to say I know these players and I want to give thanks to them for helping me out in basketball and my family matters: Lenerd Myles, Carl Davis, Reggie Jordan, Alonzo Verge, Kenny Davis, Ronnie Fields, Michael Hermon, Sherel Ford, Michael Finley, Donnie Boyce, Randy Brown, Kevin Garnett, Paul M. Pherson, Jimmy Sanders, Q. Dillard and the whole family, the Irvin family, Daddy Agee and Arthur Agee, Reggie Davis, Andrell Hoard, William Keys, Monte O'Quin, Reggie Smith, Kiwane Garris, Antwoine Walker, Brian Notree, Donald Whiteside, Lekieth Henderson, Kim Williams, Nate Driggers, Korry Billups, Jowan Howard, Nazi Mohammed, Townsend Orr, Kenny Prat, Brice Drew, Shawn Kemp, Pete Meyers, Jacque Vaughn, Linton Johnson, Shannon Brown, Will Bynum, Tony Allen, Cory McGetty, Rafer Alston, and Marcus White. If I left anybody out,

41

I'm sorry, but you know who you are and I promise you when you walk up to me I will acknowledge you unlike most stars who forget where they came from. I'm never going to forget the people who helped me.

I'm glad to say I know these ballplayers because they have been a part of my growth in life and sports. I hope they continue to be successful in their careers. You must always remember to never forget where you came from, and to give back. "Giving back is the rent you pay for your time here on earth" (Terrie Williams).

I also had a great opportunity to meet Pete Babcock, vice president and general manager of the Atlanta Hawks. He later became a good friend, along with Mitch Kupchack, Wally Walker, and Pat Williams, all of whom are presidents and general managers for the Los Angeles Lakers, Seattle Supersonics, and Orlando Magic, respectively. When I played basketball in the Pro-Am Tournament I did really well so they invited me to their NBA camps even though I didn't make the team. It was a dream come true.

In college I never got enough playing time to show what I could really do. My athletic director, Dr. Vivian F. Fuller, used to tell me my time would come and if it wasn't playing basketball at NEIU, then God had other plans for me. That meant a lot to me, coming from such a sweet and respected woman like Dr. Fuller because she didn't have to care.

I kept the faith and, as soon as the season was over and I started doing well in the Pro-Am games, I began to get calls from everywhere to come and try out for different NBA clubs. People started telling me I looked like superstar Shawn Kemp. Everybody called me Baby Kemp, a name I got back in 1990 because we resemble each other so much.

Not only was I good enough to try out for an NBA team, but I came close to making it too. I tried out for four different teams, although I wasn't supposed to even be there according to some people, but I ended up getting the last laugh. Randy Brown, Chicago Bulls guard and a buddy of mine, helped me out tremendously when I played in the tournaments at Leclaire Courts. He gave me great advice to improve my game.

I thank God for giving me the talent to play sports because it helped my career at Northeastern go by quickly. I was lucky to have graduated from that institution with two degrees, one in psychology and one in speech performing arts/communications. I had particular trouble with psychology, statistics, and social psychology lab. It was my second time taking these classes with the same two instructors, and they had already failed me the previous semester.

I felt these instructors were not giving me the grades I deserved. Have you ever spent all night on a paper for which you expected an A grade, but you got a C or a D? I questioned these teachers and was told my work wasn't good enough. I would have rather had them come right out and say they didn't like me!

I explained to the teachers that I had five kids and was doing the best I could. I never missed class—sometimes I even brought the kids to school with me. The instructor's reply to me was that no one had told me to have all those kids. I held back my anger, hoping one day to tell off both instructors. They seemed to be in cahoots to fail me, even though I was doing all the material the class required.

I suspected they were jealous or suspicious of a young black man with five children trying to get a degree. They probably expected me to rob somebody or drop out of college. It was difficult to face them every day, but my children kept me going.

Therefore, I was determined to reach my dreams. Reputation is what others think about you, but character is what you think about yourself. While others may refer to me as a basketball star, grad student, motivational speaker, author, businessman, or philanthropist, the title I treasure above all else is "**father**."

Nate III and his baby sister Nicosia having fun in her crib.

Nicosia teaching herself to walk.

Nicosia having the time of her life, eating.

Nate being a newcomer to basketball and Nicosia teaching herself the wave of the new millennium, health care.

Nicosia and Nate III thinking "hard" about their next move.

Nate III and Nicosia trying to figure out where "the new-comer," Shaquille, came from.

Shaquille making his way into the world with eyes to see into the future.

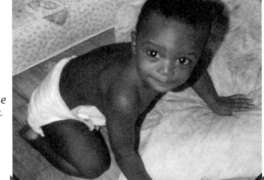

46

Christmas in the Henry household.

Nate III already assuming "the big brother role" to his younger sister Nicosia and brother Shaquille.

My deepest thoughts are on the security of my family as we grow.

(left to right) Nate III, Shaquille and Nicosia all believe they are number one, but Shaquille has a trick for them.

(right) Nicosia Henry, a.k.a. "P.B." [Pretty Beast]–future WNBA Super Star. Perhaps the first female to go pro and make WNBA history straight out of high school.

(below) Nate III heading to the Olympics/NBA out of Bolingbrook High School. After him, his sisters and brothers.

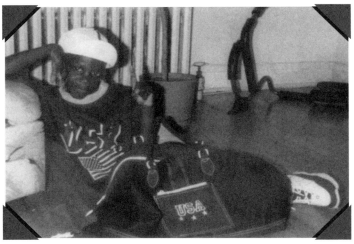

Adjusting to Developmental Dilemmas

Our fourth child Jocqui was born on February 24, 1995. Although many people would question why we kept having children, we didn't. God meant for us to have these children or He wouldn't have given them to us.

Jocqui's first breakthrough for his future in modeling.

It is most people's attitudes about having children that make a young girl reluctant to tell her parents if she finds herself pregnant. Guys are more nervous inside about how they are going to support their newborn baby. They don't worry too much how their parents are going to react. Guys question themselves in ways such as, I'm about to be a young father now, am I ready for this? They keep this information to themselves and do what they have to do to take care of their baby. A man having a baby is going to be a changed man because of it.

49

Most men are very protective of their kids. Of course, there are some who don't take care of their responsibilities; these men will be punished by God. It doesn't matter if you never speak to the mother of your child, you must always take care of your children. And never take out your problems on your child.

Four months after Jocqui was born, we had to rush him to the hospital because of a protrusion of a body part, a hernia. I knew something was wrong because Jocqui would always cry for no reason. During those first months Jocqui wouldn't eat and when we were able to get him to eat he threw the food up. It was very frustrating because the doctor couldn't figure out what was wrong with him.

Every night I heard my baby crying while the other kids were sleeping, and I couldn't do anything about it. He would look into our eyes begging for us to do something, but Nicosia and I were clueless. Nicosia would start crying and I would get mad and start doing pushups to calm myself down. I thought Jocqui was going to die. Finally, I decided I wasn't going to let my baby keep suffering.

I put on my coat and bundled him up, walking 2 miles to the hospital before a cab driver stopped and gave me a ride. The buses had already stopped running because it was so late and the car broke down. The doctors there discovered Jocqui had a hernia. When they told me they would have to operate, I broke down and started crying. I called Nicosia and explained the situation to her. She was upset and worried this type of surgery could affect Jocqui's ability later in life to father children. I told her we had to keep praying and put our trust in God. As Les Brown said, "As long as you put God first you'll never come in second."

I was so nervous and upset I was constantly questioning the nurses. I finally calmed down before they threw me out of the hospital. An hour later the doctor came out and told me the operation was successful and Jocqui was going to be fine. I was so relieved, I immediately called my wife and told her she could stop worrying. Our baby would be home tomorrow. We both started thanking God, for once again He hadn't let us down.

The next day the other children went to the nursery and I stayed home to watch Jocqui. It was so much better this time; he was able to go right to sleep after he ate his oatmeal. I was soaking in the bathtub thinking about all I'd been through. *Never Anything Too Easy* was in my thoughts. One day it seemed like I might lose my boy, and now there he was, sleeping in the next room. And people say there isn't a God. I know He's real.

Its like Daddy Agee tells me all the time: "Nate, when God bless it, look out because can't nobody do it like Him. Sometimes, Nate, you just have to be patient and let God work. He knows what He's doing; that's why He's God." For those of you who don't know who Daddy Agee is, he's the father of Arthur Agee who starred in the movie *Hoop Dreams*.

I am very close to the Agee family and often go to church with them. Mommy Agee is so sweet and loves my children. Arthur and I often play ball together at the East Bank Club or at Northeastern Illinois University. He is so strong and determined to make it no matter what. Arthur reminds me a lot of myself. People say he can't make it to the NBA, but that just makes him work harder. And you better believe he's headed to the NBA.

Almost a year after Jocqui was born, Nicosia and I had another baby on March 23, 1996.

Ashanti Henry was born almost five months earlier than the expected date and weighed just 2 pounds. The doctors said she might not live and they would have to keep her at the hospital for at least a month to monitor her. We were extremely upset by this.

Don't get me wrong—we understood the procedure and they had to keep our baby until she gained some weight. As parents, though, we wondered why this had happened. Nicosia had taken her daily iron and vitamins and ate plenty of vegetables. We researched the matter to identify any problems that could be prevented in the future.

We finally got a call from the hospital saying our baby weighed 5 pounds and was no longer in the danger zone. We ran out of the house so fast we both forgot our house keys. Luckily the landlord was there when we arrived back from the hospital. I remember kissing Ashanti so much Nicosia was angry. I didn't pay her any mind though, for the burden from my heart was lifted. I love my children so much; it is astonishing to me how they are developing.

One day Nicosia went down to her college to pick up her daily assignments because she wrote for the University Illinois Chicago newspaper at the time. She wasn't supposed to be out of the house because she had just had a baby and the doctor told her to rest for six to eight weeks, and she only did a month of that.

While she was gone, I was planning a surprise party for her because she did such a good job of delivering our fifth baby. It was my way of saying "thank you" for giving me another child. The party was just supposed to be for my wife, me, and the children. I had to go to the store to get the party favors and cake. My plan was to feed the kids and put them to bed, then go out quickly and get everything. The store was just four blocks away and I was gone for a little more than 20 minutes, but before I left I made sure the kids were sound asleep.

I was on my way back from the store and somebody called my name. I looked up and it was Nicosia hanging out of our apartment window, screaming, "The kids are gone and the house has been torn apart!" I dropped the bags and raced upstairs. I started calling around and looking for clues as to where our children were. I noticed three new messages on the answering machine. One was from our landlord saying he needed me to let him in because the apartment had to be inspected that day. I had forgotten it was inspection day for the building. He had opened up our apartment to find the children there alone and had called the police. Now you can guess where the other two messages came from.

I ended up spending 18 hours in jail. The story was all over the news: "Father leaves kids alone for six hours." This was a lie because I wasn't even gone for 30 minutes.

When I got out, Nicosia told me DCFS had the kids. We needed to find someone to keep the children until our court date. I called my father and he already had seen the news. The first thing that came out of his mouth was, "Son, it's going to be all right." He asked if there was anything he could do. Once again my father was there for me. He called DCFS and after they did a background check on him, he was able to pick up the children the next day after they were "rounded up."

I knew they must have been scared to death since they were apart for the first time. I knew what I did was wrong, but DCFS could have at least given the kids to Nicosia because she didn't have anything to do with it. She hadn't even been there when this happened. I was ready to take all the heat for what I had done; I just wanted my kids back home. "God grant me the serenity, to accept the things I cannot change, courage to change the things I can, and the wisdom to know the difference." The Serenity prayer helped me keep my sanity.

We went through the court process, and the judge saw we *were* fit parents and gave our kids back to us. We had been without them for a week—I tell you, there were some very long days without our kids in the house. When you're used to hearing all that noise from your kids and someone suddenly takes them away from you, it saddens you deeply.

I know all over the nation there are millions of families that go through this type of situation. This may be true in many cases, whether the family is financially stable or the parents just make mistakes. That still gives the court no right to take away what you've brought biologically into this world. "You must operate on the assumption that, all I know is what I have learned and all I have learned is not all there is to know" (Myles Munroe and Celeste Johnson).

I know in my case I made a big mistake and I've paid for it dearly. But I love my kids to death and the thought of not having them with me hurts like hell. Something has got to be done about the system. That's why I share my experiences with you—many times parents end up doing the wrong thing because the judge has awarded their kids to the state. Sometimes this results in death of the parents, for they will never be the same without their children. The kids are stressed and not doing well in school because they miss their parents.

You would think after going through all this beauracracy, almost losing our children, Nicosia and I would have grown closer.

One of Jocqui's most joyful moments, strolling through the house.

Jocqui realizes that he holds the keys to the world.

Coming home from the hospital, Jocqui still feels the effects of the operation.

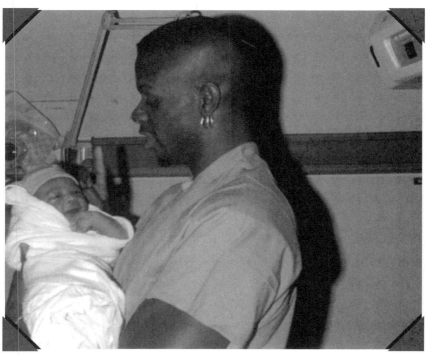

A father's joy: holding my newborn baby daughter Ashanti.

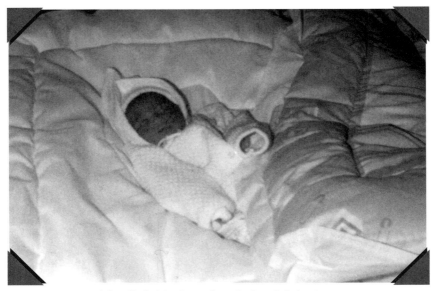

Ashanti's first day home from the hospital, she sleeps.

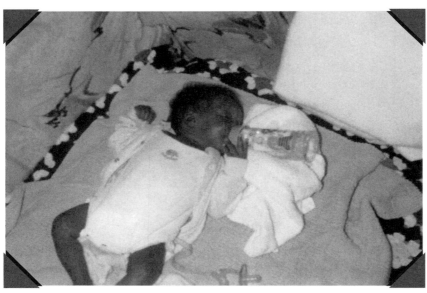

Ashanti after a hard day's work.

CHAPTER 8

Untold Truth of Marital Departure

Mrs. Nicosia Johnson-Henry was having an affair with some guy in Bellwood, Illinois, while pregnant with my baby. I probably could have handled her cheating on me but she broke our marriage vows. I don't blame the guy at all because I'm not a "player hater" but here you have this loving husband and father who just got through fighting the system so they wouldn't take our kids away from us. Meanwhile she was planning to leave and take my kids anyway.

Yes, people, what you thought was a nuclear family in the making was actually an atomic bomb blown apart by a lady's lust for another man. What I'm about to say hurts me deeply because I never imagined Nicosia and I would not be together, let alone all five of my kids would be taken away. I was sick and couldn't understand why Nicosia would do this when she knew I was a black man who survived all the inescapable struggles of life. "You must be patient, allowing others to fall and grow, understanding that potential is more valuable than behavior" (Myles Munroe and Celeste Johnson).

On August 10, 1996, Nicosia and I got into an argument about my picking her up from work. I had a basketball game at

1:00 that day, which wouldn't be over until 3:00. She wanted me to pick her up from work at 2:00. I suggested she wait an hour for me or take the bus. The kids didn't get out of daycare until 4:00 and then we could have picked them up together.

She went into a frenzy and said crazy things. "Fuck you, Nate. You don't have to pick me or the kids up. I'll get somebody who will come and get us. You just stay there and play that bullshit basketball game." That day, she left me and broke up our family for good.

Thinking about it, I feel I didn't do anything wrong at all. It was just her way of finding an excuse to leave me and go live with that other man. It was like she knew I wasn't going to be able to pick her up on time. She had it all planned out with the guy waiting on the side to take her and my kids to his home.

After my game I stayed up there at the park and watched the other games to cool off. After all, she already told me she had somebody coming to get her and the kids. I waited until 7:00 that evening and called home, hoping she had calmed down but the phone just rang and rang. I quickly dashed home.

I ran upstairs and found the kids' dresser drawers left open with all their clothes missing. I then went into my room and saw she had taken all of her things as well. I called around everywhere asking if anybody had seen Nicosia and the kids, but nobody knew anything. Her family and friends didn't like me anyway so it was easy for them to keep it a secret.

I looked everywhere and tried everything, even lying to the police saying they were kidnaped but the police said they couldn't do anything unless they were gone for 24 hours. The night came; I couldn't sleep. It was like a half of me was missing and the other half was gradually deteriorating for she had left me without a clue. I was sick and didn't know what to do. A week went by and I still didn't hear from her.

My sister Lenette would tell me, "Junior, don't worry about it. It's going to be all right." My sister gave me a big word of encouragement when she said, "Junior, she calls you all the time."

"What do you mean?" I asked.

"Does someone call you and hang up the phone?" I said yes, it happened a lot. Lenette explained, "That's Nicosia deciding whether she should come back home or not."

"Net, why is she playing games like that? I can't take this shit for much longer. I'm about to kill myself." Lenette begged me not to do anything foolish, reminding me that I had my children to live for.

It still puzzles me to this day how my wife could mess up what we worked so hard to get. Nicosia had it made. I had mapped out our life so well she wouldn't even have to work. I remember Nicosia telling me she was tired of working at Jewel Grocery Store, and I asked her to hold on a little longer. I was thinking of a plan that would have us living comfortably, and at the same time Nicosia wouldn't have to work. I had hooked Nicosia up so sweet her own parents and friends were questioning her, asking if I was selling drugs. Even my own family was asking the same foolish questions.

I had set it up so Nicosia didn't have to do anything but concentrate on completing her college degree. I had bought her a 7,000-dollar diamond ring, a 61-inch television, and a 6,000-dollar marble bed set. I really loved this woman. She was my queen, my earth, and I was planning on being with her for the rest of my life.

Nicosia was in awe after receiving these gifts. I was trying to live life right and productive, not wrong and disruptive. I told her this was God blessing us for working so hard. It was my way of apologizing for when I used to be one of the men who hit women; but that had been a long time ago when I didn't know any better.

In 1989 and 1990 Nicosia and I used to always get into fights. I know I was wrong to hit her, but I was young and sat in jail two days for it. Now I know that any man who hits a lady is a weak man. I got on my knees and begged the Lord for forgiveness and asked Him to help me so I wouldn't do this again.

59

I couldn't justify why Nicosia and I had become so angry at one another. Dr. Charles McCloskey says, "Anger is a normal physiological response to a particular situation. It's a human emotion that we all have, and it's very healthy if we know how to let it out." McCloskey also says, "The problem comes in because people have a tendency to hold that anger in instead of dealing with it, and letting it build up. That's when people have a tendency *to explode.*"

Rich Higinbotham, a social worker who specializes in anger management, says, "Anyone who is persistent and determined can learn to handle their anger in a better way" (Tracy Boyd, *Chicago Sun-Times*, November 12, 1999). It's hard for me to talk about this but I want you all to know what *Never Anything Too Easy* is all about. Like I said, I've been through a lot.

The problem with this is when you share your life story with the public, people tend to think you can't change. When the ladies find out you once used to hit a woman they start giving you this label as a "woman beater," or say you're less of a man. Not all ladies think or say these things; a lot of women understand a man's problem, especially a black man. I'm not saying, ladies, if your man is beating on you every day you should stay with him. No! Get out of that relationship as soon as you can. I wasn't doing those things and believe me, Nicosia wouldn't have stayed with me six years if I was that bad.

I know some people are going to try to shoot me down when they see me, because they can't wait to hate. These are character killers. This disease is bigger than AIDS and growing rapidly every day. The scary part is that scientists haven't even found a cure or drug to slow it down.

I loved Nicosia deeply and couldn't understand why she left me like she did. It was already hard enough taking care of five kids with both of us going to school. I truly believed she loved her husband.

I remembered Nicosia's birthday in 1995. I picked the kids up first that day, then Nicosia. We went to a car dealership and we traded our year-old Honda in for a Land Cruiser. Nicosia was shocked and wondered how I pulled this off when we both had bad credit. I just worked it because I wanted my baby to have a birthday she'd never forget.

Well, by now you're probably wondering where I got the money to buy all that stuff for Nicosia? I used school loans, public aid checks, project chance checks, and so forth. I'm very smart when it comes to budgeting and handling money, and even though neither of us had jobs, I *manipulated the system*. All we had to do was maintain a C average to stay eligible for financial aid, which in turn let us take out school loans we didn't have to pay back until we were finished with school entirely. We could receive our bachelor's, master's, and doctorate degrees as long as we kept getting deferment forms filled out.

I had it all running smoothly until Nicosia messed it up. People thought we were rich. On Saturdays the kids would go to ballet classes in a Land Cruiser. I gave Nicosia five kids and anything else a twenty-one-year-old woman could ask for, but she broke my heart and left me for another man and got pregnant by him while still being married. Nicosia committed adultery.

My first reaction was to go kick the guy's ass, but I knew I probably would have killed him and ended up in jail. Plus, it wasn't his fault.

Nicosia got orders of protection taken out on me so I couldn't see my children. Every time I went to court, she wouldn't show up, but she would take out another order of protection. She kept this up for five months, I couldn't see my kids and it was driving me insane. I got to the point where I hated her. All I ever wanted to do was be a family man and give my kids the best life ever with two parents.

After that, there was nothing left for me. People would say, Nate, you have your whole life ahead of you. You have psychology and communication degrees. You're a smart, young black man. But I was missing a critical part of my life and everything else didn't seem to matter. My kids were the biggest inspiration that I had. I forgot what Celeste Johnson said: "Things may happen around you and things may happen to you, but the most important things are the things that happen in you!"

In order to clear my head, I called my friend, John, up one day and we went for a drive. It just so happened he took me on the West Side of Chicago near where Nicosia's father lived. I saw the truck I bought her for her birthday in front of the house. I told my boy to stop the car.

I got out, knocked on the door and her father came to the door. I asked politely, "Can I see my children?" He replied, "Don't you have an order of protection against you?" He told me to get the hell away from his house, I snapped and was about to go through the house and look for my kids, but first I would have beaten his ass for disrespecting me. He threatened to call the police. My friend convinced me to leave. It was a very difficult thing to do, knowing my children, whom I hadn't seen in five months, were inside.

Nicosia was right there, and she could have let me see my babies. I never meant to cause my kids any pain. I love you Nate, Theresa, Shaquille, Jocqui, and Ashanti. I want you all to be very close and never let anybody come between you for you all are the real Henry kids. You went through a lot at an early stage in your lives, but it's only going to make you mentally tough, powerful, and distinguished.

I used to beep Nicosia 20 times a day begging her to come back home. A lot of times I'd be crying on her voice mail because I missed my kids so much. She never returned my calls, and this continued for a month until one day she decided to call back. I was sitting in the living room looking out of the window thinking the apartment was so empty and quiet without my kids running around. She called and told me to stop calling. We were through.

She told me she let her friends listen to my crazy voice mail messages. The man she was with made 28,000 dollars a year and I didn't have a job. I asked her if this was all about money.

"You'd rather have our kids suffer not seeing their father because of money?" I asked. "If that's the case, I will get a job."

She said it was too late for that and she was happy where she was.

I told her I had potential to make a lot of money, but she didn't care. Then I reminded her we had bills stacked up to the ceiling and unpaid rent.

"That's not my problem, it's your problem, Nate," she replied.

"Nicosia," I said, "we put our money together in your bank account."

"Oh well, Nate, tough luck," she giggled.

"Nicosia, I trusted you, that's why I put all the money in your name."

Then she hit me with a low blow. "Nate, make it the best way you can. As far as I'm concerned, my kids don't have a father because you will never see them again." CLICK!

My ex-wife took everything, including our kids.

CHAPTER 9

Many Fractured Wonders

I asked myself the same questions every day: Why did my Black Queen snatch the spine out of my back to leave me leaning over like that? Did she forget who helped her get back in college when they kicked her out? Who is really inside her making her act like this? Where are my children? When am I going to see them again? How am I going to get them back? *Never Anything Too Easy* once again was an obstacle I had to get over, but I still haven't been able to answer these six questions.

As I was going through this, my mind was on my little brother who was locked up for hanging with the wrong crowd. I cried each day he was in there; I didn't know if he was strong enough to handle being in his cell 23 hours a day. I sometimes wished I could do the bid for him. I prayed every day hoping God would release him, but it didn't happen. Between this and my kids being taken away I was on the edge, waiting to hit rock bottom.

It was written like this from the first day: I was chosen to be the one to go through all these predicaments to help young men, as well as older men, who have been through the same things I have. And to let women know it's not right to put a good man through this. I was ordained to write this book and be the motivation you need to get you through your days of worries. This world has a whole lot of questions with no answers. Had God not taken me through a hard life I wouldn't have been able to speak to you. And what I'm about to tell you goes against society's rules and is out of the norm for some people.

I met a white woman, a *Jewish* white woman. I know what you all are thinking—especially you, Nicosia. But this is your fault; it hurts doesn't it? I assure you she is not pregnant—yet! How many of you who read the previous part let your prejudice come out?

It's okay. I don't blame you. I blame society and your parents for not educating you better on the subject. At some point in time people are going to have to get off that racial inequality. We're all from the same biological species. I realize some of you are deep into whatever your beliefs are, and I respect that but don't knock me. My theme is, "As long as there is life there's hope."

The girl's name is Nicole—almost the same as my ex-wife. My mother from the heavens sent her to me, right when it looked like everything was gone. Maybe this will help people not to look at color but at a person's heart. Don't misunderstand me; I love my black sisters and I know some of them wouldn't have put me through what my ex-wife did. At the time when I was in my darkest hour there wasn't a black woman in sight. I was closing in on death, begging for help, but still no one answered. Then came Nicole to rescue me. I didn't see color. I saw a woman extending her hand out to me.

She was like an angel sent from the heavens, letting me stay with her and her brother at their apartment. She bought me food, helped me get through the remaining part of school, gave me money, let me use her car, and sat up late hours consoling me while I was trying to cope with the absence of my children.

Her parents were totally against what Nicole was doing for me; they were very prejudiced. They asked Nicole, "What do you see in that black boy? He's nothing but a loser." Nicole would stand her ground and say I wasn't a loser, that I had two degrees, was very smart in school, and an excellent basketball player. Nicole's father is a dream buster. "Dream busters—get them out of your life, they will deplete your energy" (Les Brown).

She didn't tell them about my kids because they couldn't handle the situation. They paid the bills for Nicole while she was in school, and they were already threatening to cut her off. They figured since they were rich upper-class people Nicole should be with somebody the same. People would tell her parents they saw her daughter with a black guy and they would hate that. Our own friends would get mad as well.

Black women would see us together and start shaking their heads. They would say things like, "What a shame how black men be going to them white women!" Let me tell you something, people with the prejudiced minds. I don't care what you think, calling me a sell out. When I was left on the curve of death there wasn't a black person in sight trying to help me, but yet you all want to sit up here and criticize. When God comes, I will be judged accordingly. Until then, you just try to live right and be ready when He comes or you might end up going to hell faster than I. To Nicole I say, thank you for being there and if we don't work out in the future you will always be special in my life.

As time passed I began to get stronger but still was weak when people asked me about my children. I would lie and say they were doing fine. Later on that day I would walk to the lake and cry. I missed my children in every single way that's possible, and ways I didn't even know were possible. How could Nicosia Johnson do this to our kids? I could hear them crying out, "Daddy, Daddy, where are you?" But I couldn't answer them back.

One night about 3:00 AM I got a call from Nicosia telling me to rush to Loyola Hospital because something had happened to baby Ashanti. Quickly, I rushed out of the house, jumped into the car, and sped to the hospital doing about 100 miles per hour.

I got to the emergency room and asked for my baby. They asked who I was. I told them I was the father. All the time I was praying to God, Please don't let my baby be dead! They took me into her room and Ashanti was lying there, screaming in pain. I looked on in shock—my baby's leg was broken in half! The doctors were sticking pins in her leg to keep it together, which made her cry even louder. Tears were streaming down my face. Although I was happy to see her, I wished it could have been under different circumstances.

I was so angry and ready to kill Nicosia, her boyfriend, and whoever else allowed this to happen. I ran out of the room looking for Nicosia all over the hospital, but I couldn't find her anywhere. She was lucky that night because there is no telling what I would have done to her.

Since I couldn't locate Nicosia, I looked on the doctor's chart and saw the address and phone number under which she registered. I called and Nicosia's boyfriend answered. I didn't waste any time telling him I was the father of Nicosia's children. I asked what had happened to my baby.

He explained he had been in the kitchen and Nicosia in the bathroom while the kids were playing in the bedroom. Ashanti was on the top of the bunk bed left unattended. He then said one of the kids pushed her off of the bed and that's when she broke her leg. He was calm and coming at me in the right way, but of course, it wasn't his kid in the hospital.

"Why in the hell did you leave her on the bed by herself, let alone the top of a bunk bed?" I asked. He then said he didn't even know the baby was on the bed and that Nicosia was supposed to be watching them.

Eventually, I saw Nicosia and shook my head in disbelief. I told her I was just talking with her guy friend and didn't even bother to ask her why she left me and took the kids. I went on and told her he was just as stupid as she.

I believe there are behaviors for which apologies are appropriate. There also are behaviors where apologies are not appropriate or sufficient. These are issues of forgiveness. Nicosia wasn't even going to call me. The only reason she did call was because DCFS asked her where the father was. They told her she could lose the children if her story didn't prove to be true.

They interviewed me and asked me a series of questions about Nicosia; if she was a fit mother, why we were not together, if I see the kids, and so forth. I could have done Nicosia wrong and got back at her for the things she did to me by lying to DCFS. The repercussions of that could have meant the loss of my children to the system and that was the only reason I supported Nicosia's story. I didn't want my children to be without both of their parents. Once again DCFS closed the case and let us keep our children.

Because of this accident, Nicosia began to let me spend time with the kids. She started letting me pick up the kids every three weeks. At first it was difficult because we hadn't seen each other for so long. My children loved for me to pick them up, but they hated for me to drop them off.

Nate, Nikki, and Shaquille, my three oldest children, would always ask, "Daddy, you're not taking us home to Mommy are you?" I would respond with "yes" and explain that I would be back the next week to pick them up again. They started crying, saying, "We don't want to go back over there with Mommy. We want to live with you, Daddy. We miss you." Those were some of the hardest moments.

I looked into their eyes when it was time for me to drop them off and just tried to hold the tears back while each one of them gave me a hug. They went into the house and as I was leaving they would look out the window waving at me with tears coming down their faces. When I drove off, I couldn't hold the tears back. I wanted to fulfill my children's request to live with me, but I couldn't because their mother wouldn't allow it.

Knowing I had to wait three weeks to see them again depleted my energy. I knew I had to stay focused in order to sustain myself for the next 21 days. The next time I picked them up they were so happy to see me, my youngest boy, Jocqui, almost got hit by a car trying to get to his daddy. I loaded them up and we drove off singing church songs. I was so busy playing with them at every stoplight, I didn't notice the stitches on the back of Shaquille's head.

When we arrived at the apartment I was attending to my two youngest babies, Jocqui and Ashanti, because they had been gone so long it was harder for them to have an idea of who their father was or what he was like. They were little babies when all this took place between their mother and me. Little Nate, Nikki, and Shaquille were playing basketball on the rim I bought for them. I noticed Shaquille was grabbing the back of his head. I looked and saw these stitches on the back of his head and almost fainted. I asked Shaquille what happened. Nate and Nikki explained they were jumping on the bed and Shaquille fell on his head.

My heart started beating rapidly and my hands became sweaty. I stopped what I was doing and picked up the phone to call Nicosia. I must have left 10 messages on her voice mail. Why hadn't she called me and let me know my baby had a serious injury? I was saddened the whole weekend the children and I were together. I knew my little boy was scared and hurt and I hadn't been there for him. I cried in front of Shaquille and let him know that his head would be all right and to be careful not to play so rough.

I sat back and thought about all the things Nicosia did to me. It made me wonder if I would ever get married again. It's hard for me to place my trust in another woman. There are some good women still out there, but would I be able to open up again? I have faith God will send me a blessing and she will be just like the poem my good friend from college Thebes Napata Assyeria wrote. It goes like this:

Lord give me the wisdom and knowledge
to learn how to eject the negative
>*world perception life.*
As complicated thoughts cross my mind,
my visualization clouds as they
>*rise to the ceiling.*
The scent of clouds as trees hum, how
lovely it would be.
>*Amazing vibes are brought among many*
>*spirits.*
Father lead me to a warm sincere heart.
>*As wished for a strong mind, body, and*
>*spirit with an unusual intellect.*
May both become powerful in thy name,
some laugh while others cry.
>*Don't let my misunderstanding divide*
>*the love which was once by.*

One of my other close friends and former Northeastern Illinois basketball players, Robert Silo, helped me to orchestrate my life. He would break it down to me why some women do the things they do and how we as men must be forgiving. I didn't understand that concept but now I see what he meant. Some women don't know the ways of the world and this is why they do negative things to men.

At NEIU we had what you call "a session." Included in this session was myself aka Baby Kemp, Andrell Hoard aka Highlight, William Keys aka Lil Crucial, Brian Rogers aka Buc Lord, Kaylon Coleman aka Smooth/Footwork, and last but not least Gene Casperd aka Promoter. We would all sit down every day and pick a topic to discuss. Highlight would usually kick it off. The next thing you know everybody would start vibing off one another's experiences. Sometimes it would get really intense. One day the subject was about women. Baby Kemp kicked that one off.

Everyone started getting personal with the others in the session, and some got mad and took the situation to heart. Men were sharing parts of themselves that others wouldn't have dreamed they went through. When it came to my turn, I talked about marriage and children. I wasn't even halfway through the story when tears started coming down my face. I had never cried before during a session.

Those sessions were extremely powerful, enhancing my desire to produce a movie about my life. Being a native of Chicago a movie has always been a thought. The movie will be named *Never Anything Too Easy* like the book. My future plans are then to produce a second book followed by another movie. The life of Nathaniel J. Henry growing up has no doubt been hard, but life is what you make it. I think the divorce from Nicosia was the hardest thing I had to swallow because of the children and how the whole situation happened. Even though Nicosia and I had our ups and downs, the past cannot be forgotten or forsaken. I hope she has a healthy and happy life and wish no harm or danger upon her. No matter what, children (including my own) need both parents, if possible, to survive in the world. This increased my curiosity to understand relationships and why Nicosia and other women treat men as badly as they do.

It was a nightmare to get the call to come to the hospital to find out my daughter Ashanti's leg was broken.

Although visitation wasn't often, the time we got to spend with one another was irreplaceable.

CHAPTER 10

Enlightening the Opposition

I have a psychology degree and decided to put my knowledge to work by conducting a study. Looking at relationships, it is amazing the different emotions that are felt. My question has always been, Why does it have to be so hard? The answer that I came up with was one that I have devoted a lot of my time to research.

I conducted a study that consisted of 200 men and women. I asked all of them the same questions, which were all relationship-based. These questions helped me to see how differently women and men look at relationships. Women say they want a man who is sweet, kind, affectionate, and loves their children. Then why do they go for a man with money over a man who will treat them right? Women find it's more of a challenge to be with someone who doesn't show them affection. When women do not feel their man is treating them right they are inclined to try to figure out why. The mystery of the answer is intriguing to most women. Women find themselves in an uncomfortable position yet, they still persist in staying in that situation. The old saying "nice guys finish last" is true.

Basically what a women says and what she means are two different things. They do say that after they are interested in a man who shows them just a little bit of affection they are willing to try to find ways to compensate for what they really want from a man. It is extremely difficult for a woman to admit she wants to be with a man who is rude, embarrassing, or even harmful. It stems from a woman's childhood when she is taught to find a good man and make sure he treats her right. Parents want their children to have the best of everything, including their future partners. Women subconsciously know the type of man they find intriguing.

In society's eyes, these men are looked at negatively. Women always listen to their friends' opinions. The problem with females is that they listen and follow what their friends say. Women try very hard to establish friendships that will last forever. They take the word "forever" to the furthest point and manipulate this. If a man says he will stay with his women forever she will believe him no matter if it is true or not. This is because women have a need to feel wanted and needed. They feel that when a man can say the word "forever," it could never be a lie. In their hearts women know that all people in this world lie, but since they want to believe this so badly they do not think of the consequences. That is why women fall in love so quickly.

When a man tells a woman he loves her, he has hit the most sensitive part of a woman's body and soul. Those words can be more powerful than death. He has taken over her entire brain. After that point it is not an unbelievable concept that a woman would stay with a man just because of a few words. In a relationship a woman will trust a man and give her heart and soul to just hear those few words. Why? I found that a woman's need to feel comfort and security is the most important feeling to a woman. When a man can just sit and hold a woman, she feels nothing in the world could hurt them. The strength of two arms can be more powerful than eternal life.

Speaking from a man's point of view I feel these things have a proper time and place. In a woman's subconscious mind, she wants to have these feelings all day, every day. The affection that is felt by the simple touch of a hand or the arms wrapped around a person's body could move the world. This is why so many women hate to even think of another woman touching their man. When they feel that they have given a man their heart and soul and especially their body, they don't ever want to see their man come close to another lady.

A challenge to a woman is what adds excitement to their lives. A man can only do so much; women need to fulfill their sense of security and one way to do that is to see if another man finds her attractive and sexy. This is what leads to a habit of cheating in some women. When a woman feels she has a man and is secure in a relationship, that is her ticket to go out and cheat. A woman is able to go out with her friends and flirt to see if she still looks appealing to other people. Although not all women cheat, there are females who need to feel that other men still find them attractive. Once they see that this is true they are able to go back to their man and appreciate him more.

Those who do cheat are often just insecure, and insecurity is the recourse of a weak mind. Some women think their man is cheating on them so they feel they should do the same. Since everyone is human and we all make mistakes, it is not an unforgivable thing for people to cheat. If a woman has a requirement to feel wanted and needed and does not receive it at home, her first instinct is to go and find that feeling somewhere else.

In some cases some women use sex as a way to get close to a man. In their eyes it is like a signed consent form to be a large part of their lives. It's not necessarily the act of sex that brings them closer. It is the fact that they feel they have given their body, so the man owes them something in return. Usually they want money or affection to be shown all the time. Men do not think of sex in the same way as women do because they don't want to think of it as an emotional tie.

When and if a woman who has cheated decides to tell her significant other about what she has done, she has to arrange the perfect scenario. This usually consists of a romantic candlelight dinner or a special outfit that will turn a man on. With these tactics a woman is appealing to a man's sensitive and sexual side. When they are preoccupied with what the woman is wearing or doing they are not really concentrating on what is coming out of her mouth. Women will come up to a man and begin to kiss and caress him. This distraction usually comes in a form of massage, extensive disclosure of emotion, and deep stares into the eyes.

After they have had what seems to be the best sex ever the woman will say, Honey, I have something I need to tell you. The man with a huge smile on his face while holding his woman will say, "You can tell me anything, baby."

With a crackle in her soft voice she will say that every Thursday night when she says that she is going out with the girls, she goes to a male friend's house. She immediately turns over and looks straight into her man's eyes and tells him that the sex meant nothing. She will shed a tear out of fear of abandonment.

By this point the man has more often than not gotten out of bed and just looks at his wife or girlfriend. As he looks her up and down she pulls the covers over herself and feels a sharp pain in her heart. The tears begin to roll down her face and the man, still looking at her in disappointment, does not know what to say. She begs and pleads with him to forgive her for what she has done because it was childish and stupid. Then things are said such as, "I don't need to do that anymore. I know now that you are the only man for me and there is no one in this world who can make me feel the way you do."

Grabbing onto the closest part of his anatomy, she will hold on for dear life while the tears roll down her face. She keeps on repeating, "I'm sorry, I'm sorry," until she feels better about what she did. Then if the man has still not replied to what she has just told him, she will become defensive and say things like, "At least I told you about it. Sue didn't even tell John." With that she will get up and put her clothes on.

At this point a woman feels at peace within herself even if she feels guilty about what she has done. When disclosing the evidence that her best friend did not tell her husband and she did, she feels she has more respect and love for her man. The reality is that she feels so guilty and sorry for hurting her man, she does not have any other outlets. She will go and look her man in the eyes and tell him she made a mistake and she will never do it again. "I am only human and you can't use that against me." Again she is trying to justify what she has done. If the man has exercised nonverbal communication she is more upset than she was before.

When a woman can see a look of disappointment in her man's eyes, and a piercing look of anger at the same time, she does not know what to do. She will contemplate walking out, try to hug him or kiss him, or when all else fails she will try to make love to him again. If the man allows her to get close to him, she feels that all is forgiven. The act of sex is a reminder that no matter what she did with that other man, she still came back to her man to prove her love. She tells him this experience has taught her that no other man is better than the one she has lying right next to her. At this point she is on top of her man and telling him she will do anything to make up for what she has done.

After pouring out her guilt, she gives him some sort of gift or poem she has written. This distraction helps the man to put what happened in the past. The female begins to talk about what she wants to do with him in the future. The futuristic talk changes what is directly on the mind and forms it into a whole different concept. The woman is still feeling a little uneasy with herself about what she has done, but for the moment she feels that she has made up for it temporarily by giving him a present and her body.

No relationship is perfect, nor is any human perfect, so we have to accept the things we cannot change. The next few days are a little bit uncomfortable. It feels like you are walking on pins and needles. The woman will do every possible thing to meet the needs of her man. She will cook all of his favorite

79

meals, wash all of the dishes, take out the garbage, do the laundry, and run to do his every last command. As she does all of these chores, the pain in her heart gets worse every day. The slow death will never end until she sees her man begin to trust her again and show her forgiveness.

The feelings of anger, love, disappointment and rejection set into the brain and take over her whole soul. She begins to miss the way it used to feel when her man would embrace her in his arms and the strength of his hands as they ran up and down her spine. These little things he used to do are the things she really misses.

The problem in most relationships is communication. When a person has made a mistake, the first thing he or she tries to do is compensate for it. Most women will grab hold of their man and not let go. In reality they are making the situation worse. In a man's mind, you are the lowest thing on earth and the only thing he wants is to be as far away from you as possible.

If a couple has a physical fight it doesn't mean either is a bad person. This is just the way a person has chosen to disclose his or her feelings. Although this is a negative way of expressing emotional distress, it is the only way certain people know. "If you can't pick up the people around you, for God's sake, don't let them bring you down" (Les Brown).

No sooner will something negative happen between a couple before a woman will go and call her friends or family to talk about it. They believe this will heal the situation and these people will be able to give them advice. But it just makes the situation more complicated.

When a woman loves a man she will try to do everything right even though a man may feel that what she has done is the complete opposite. When a woman has cheated, she will try to justify what she has done. This is how heated discussions end up in physical contact. When a man tells a lady to stay away, most will continue to stick around. At this point they know they are wrong and will do anything to make up for that. One of the ways a woman tries to keep a man down is by placing restraining orders against him. If she has children, this makes the father look bad in his children's eyes.

If a man is not causing physical harm to a woman, there is no reason for a restraining order. The system is ready to believe that all men are out to stalk a woman. With all women's stories it is surprising they don't just lock men up immediately. A woman will do anything to keep a man unhappy if he is not with her. If her man is trying to better himself, there is no way a woman will let him do that without throwing some obstacles in his path.

Women feel if they can't be with him then no one should have the opportunity. By making the man go to court, he has to see the woman and therefore deal with whatever deterrents the lady tries to enforce upon him. When a man comes to terms with what a woman has done and is ready to discuss it, a woman shouldn't act like she doesn't know what she did. It takes a lot for a man to trust someone who has destroyed that trust.

If the man is considering leaving the woman, she will find some way to make him stay around. If the man and woman have children, that's the easiest way to keep him involved in her everyday life. If there are no children, women are capable of coming up with any type of action to try to keep the man from leaving them stranded.

Some women will do anything to keep from being alone. Women think about how much they want to hold their man and can't bear the thought of another woman getting within reach.

If a couple cares about one another they shouldn't make each other's life miserable. It goes back to the whole idea of a need to feel wanted and loved. If a woman is insecure, she will try hard as hell to keep a man. What women don't realize is that you can lose a man faster by trying to keep him somewhere he does not want to be. The frustration and the pain is only going to get worse if a woman proceeds to try.

Just like a woman, a man has feelings too. The men who admit to feeling pain are the ones women want to be with. They want their man to have a strong and a weak side. In seeing these two sides, a woman is more likely to feel her man is special. When women are capable of seeing a true side of a man, they are more likely to see who they really are. The most difficult thing for a woman to do is to try to figure out a man. What they do is feel them out. Women will look at all of the different activities he participates in and then will look at the different things he does to her. If he seems to be comfortable with the situation, she is more likely to try to find out his every move.

One of the ways a woman can do this is by listening to how he talks with his close buddies. When all of his friends are in the other room and a man thinks his lady is asleep, she is most likely trying to hear what her man is saying. Although the other men in the room are speaking in the conversation, her focus is on what her man has to say about other women. Most people would think that this is a sign of insecurity but it does not always have to be.

In this world women get stepped on a lot, so to protect themselves they try to find out things on their own. Like the old saying goes, "When you are looking for hurt you will find it, even if it is not there." Women feel that by trying to find something out they will be able to throw it in their man's face before he can say it himself. Most women find it hard to believe that a "good" man actually exists. The fact of the matter is that they can exist, and often they are the ones who get stepped on and hurt in the process.

In our society men are often seen as dogs, cheaters, and liars. Since everyone is a product of their environment, it is no surprise people believe these ideas. The media has contributed to these crazy notions. This is why sincere men are not looked at as serious or are treated as though they are being smooth. In retrospect, they are not doing anything wrong; they are just acting out the way they feel. Men are taught at a very young age to be strong and to not be a "sissy." What most people think that means is to not act like a girl. The point is that when your friends and your family try to influence your opinion or decision about someone, you should not believe everything you hear. You must know your purpose before you can help someone else with their purpose.

Women are usually into their friends because they need a sense of belonging. The comfort and acceptance they receive from friends helps them to deal with all of the adversity they face. Women are more than likely to tell a man how they feel before they will go and tell a woman. Men are the opposite. They will discuss their problems or concerns with their friends before they will go to their significant other. This is why ladies will listen and gain all the knowledge of the man's life. She feels that by knowing what her man says to his friends, she will know what has to be done to keep him happy.

These are things that will help her to keep her man from cheating or going out and doing something he will regret. This is all fine and good, but not all men talk to their friends about their lady. This is because if they care about their woman they don't want their friends to believe that to be the case. Unfortunately, when women overhear this type of conversation, it is viewed as negative when it is really a positive way of looking at themselves.

After hearing a conversation a woman will do one of two things; she will either be very upset with her man and try to get him back, or she will show some type of affection or emotion. A woman may take what she overheard and try to re-enact it. If she succeeds she feels a sense of accomplishment. In reality all she has done is proven to herself that her man still has feelings for her. In most cases the man already has strong feelings for his lady, and by her showing him more attention it makes him feel more secure and full of confidence.

What most women do not realize is that their man did not speak about them to try to make them improve what they were doing, but to show their friends what a good woman they have. For a lady this is a compliment, yet most times it is taken as an insult. The problem that comes about is that after being with a man for a long period of time, a lady begins to feel less desirable and less needed. In some cases this is just her being emotional, but more times than not there is another reason behind her feelings of inadequacy.

In many relationships women find themselves doing more for a man than the man is doing for them. This happens a lot with women who feel they have something to prove to their man. These feelings usually come about when there is some type of argument and one person gets mad over nothing. When you are with a person for a long time there are bound to be things that aggravate you about them. What needs to be decided is if the argument means more than the person you had it with. We as human beings always hurt the people who are closest to us. In trying to make up for that mistake, many people will try to fix everything they feel is wrong in their relationships.

Women have a knack for making a man feel that whatever has happened is all his fault. When a woman does this to a man or vice versa, it is extremely detrimental to that person's integrity. In trying to cover up for your mistakes you do what your partner asks you. For most women their men will ask them to perform some type of sexual act or other activity the woman doesn't love doing. The woman does these things to prove to her man that she loves him and is willing to do anything to keep him happy. Men are not intentionally out to hurt their partner; they just sometimes feel insecure and have to prove to themselves that their lady really is into them the way they thought.

After the whole situation takes place the woman is left feeling empty and the man is left satisfied. This is why so many women try to not be into a man—because they do not want to lose all sense of sex appeal. The only way to do this is to keep trying to make their partner happy. If that doesn't work, some women will look for someone else to give them attention. Not all women need to look for other men to fulfill their needs.

Many women will go and get their hair done or buy a sexy outfit to make themselves feel better. If a woman can look at herself in the mirror and smile, then she is ready to go on with her life. Since no one can predict the future, it is very difficult if not impossible to describe what is going on in another person's mind.

Research has found that (Hatlage 1980, Lesak 1976, Walsh 1978) women tend to use the right side of their brain more than the left side. What this means is that women are usually better at holistic thought, nonverbal processing, music ability, and spatial recognition. So what are the men good at? Men use their left side of their brain. This side is known for analytical thinking, sequential information processing, and mathematical abilities.

Looking at the two different sides of the brain, it is apparent they have many different focuses. The main difference is that women are bilateral, meaning they go from using one side of the brain to the other. This is a task men are not very good at. This is why there are so many problems in communicating with the opposite sex. Sometimes when a man is trying to tell a woman he loves her or he is thinking about her, the woman may feel he is just saying it to cover up for whatever he has done. Women interpret this as a sign of guilt.

One of the biggest problems couples have is trying to communicate to one another how they feel. When a woman acts concerned, her man thinks she is being possessive and trying to take away his freedom. Since women use the side of their brain that deals with imagination, they try to take what a man says and analyze every word. The problem with using that tactic is that men catch on very quickly to that style of thinking. Men use their analytic thought to try to figure out what their significant other is saying.

Now that we know that men and women communicate in different ways, we need to realize that some messages come across in the opposite way they were originally intended. When trying to communicate with the opposite sex, one must try to conquer all of the aspects of cognitive thought. You have to put yourself in the position of the other sex and figure out how that person might react to what you are saying. A benefit that women have being bilateral is that they don't have to work so hard at figuring out others' emotions (Begley, "Gender Differences," 1995). Women are quick to analyze everything a person tells them. Men should take that into consideration when they are trying to communicate with a female.

There is a fine line between intimacy and independence. When women want to do something, they will ask their partner if that's okay. Women see this as showing respect to their mate. Men, however, feel this is a way of taking away their independence. A man feels belittled when he asks his spouse for permission to do anything. It makes him feel he is no longer in control of the relationship. When a man feels this way, he will resist everything a woman tries to tell him. Some men want to have all of the control, so asking for help is not something that they usually do.

In order for men and women to have a successful relationship they both need to understand that the sexes are different, and so are the motives behind the behaviors. For example, when a woman is mad at her companion she will do whatever it takes to get him back. Most of the time this is done through nonverbal communication. The problem with using this kind of approach is that if you push too many buttons you can cause yourself to do more harm than good.

Women can become so enraged that the buttons they push are not the ones that produce the right response. This in turn can make a man so angry he wants to hit his spouse. It is not right for one spouse to use physical violence to get back at the other, but women as well as men need to learn how to control their tempers.

Many spouses will put the other down when they are angry. Since both partners know each other very well, they know how to hit their weak spots. For many women their weaknesses are intelligence, body size, hair, and other parts of their physical appearance. These attributes are what women get the most sensitive about. When putting someone down you believe you are showing superiority to your subordinate.

In reality all you are doing is making a fool out of yourself. When you speak like that you are doing what is called "framing." This means that what you are saying is coming right back at you as if you were looking into a mirror. You make yourself look stupid when you talk about others in a negative way because it will come right back at you when you least expect it. As you can see, putting others down does not help the situation at all. All it does is make the other person upset.

The key to a successful argument is to keep your composure. "Don't waste your time being bitter, be better" (G. Piere). What often happens is that a man will say that the discussion is over, when the woman has more to say on the topic. The best thing for a woman to do is make it short and sweet. When things become repetitive men will block out what is being said. Then you are talking to a brick wall.

To make things as easy as possible one should tell the truth to his or her spouse no matter how much it may hurt. The truth can and does hurt, but it is better to find out right away and deal with it than to wait until the truth is revealed. Women sometimes believe that lying to their spouse is for their own protection. In reality, since the truth is almost always discovered in the end, it's not worth the trouble or the pain.

A problem many ladies have is not believing their man when he says he's going out with the guys. This is a great way for him to cover up for where he is really going. Women very often say the very same thing. Women will use family members or friends to cover up their story. Both sexes can get away with these stories if they cover them extremely well. What most women will do is tell their man he is cheating because in reality *they* are.

Women are taught at a young age to keep men guessing, which is supposed to keep them interested. Sometimes this tactic works in the beginning of the relationship, but after a while these games will terminate your relationship. Women do their best to keep a man wanting them, instead of another woman. The reason for women being so overprotective is because they are sometimes insecure. It does not matter how much money they have, or how pretty they are; women always believe there is someone out there better than they are. No two people are the same; so, what may be special to one person may not be special to another.

The mistake that most women make is trying to do everything they can to impress their man. Males are human just like females; but, that does not mean that they don't need the same things. An example that always comes up is men say they don't need love or to be shown affection. Some men require less than others, but they all need it in one way or another.

Why is it that when a lady tries to show a man affection he goes on the offensive? It is due to the fact that men hate their own emotions. What I mean by "hating" is *saying* they don't like something when they really do. When a man doesn't show affection, a woman starts to hold back too and suspicion arises. When you try to convince yourself that something is going to happen, no one should be surprised when it does. Trying to control a man—or a woman—is like trying to put handcuffs on loyalty.

It is my opinion that women in today's society have changed from what they used to be. Ever since the beginning of time God created man and then women from a bone from a man's side. If you look at the word "woman" it consists of the word "man." Men were the leaders and women their counterparts. Nowadays, I think women try to be too liberated.

Women in some countries are still accustomed to the old traditional ways of life. These women are loyal to their man no matter what or who steps in their path. Their loyalty and commitment keep their man strong and give a sense of confidence that they have someone who believes in them.

In today's society women will turn a man down and play games with his head until they have gotten him "hook, line, and sinker." All they really have is a sense of accomplishment and a man they don't want. Being afraid of losing the most important thing in your life will cause any woman to play games.

Just like men, women will test the waters to see where their limits lie. It's not a crime to see what a person is all about, but it is to take it too far. Most women misinterpret the word "loyal." The word does not just apply to cheating but to supporting a man and giving him what he needs. What a woman needs to realize is that a man will commend her for standing up for him, but he won't give her praise for trying to get involved in his personal life.

Women believe that by trying to get his friends to like her, it will enhance his feelings. This type of interaction is looked upon as the most deceitful action a woman can take. Having a conversation with one of your spouse's friends is invading his space and privacy.

When a woman gets caught up in the way a man feels about her, her mind begins to race and the nightmares begin. She will first think her man is dissatisfied with her. Then she will think he's not out with his friends but with another woman. When all these emotions begin to build up, she may lose all control. Her first course of action is to impress her man by wearing something special, or to cook him a special meal—or anything to keep his mind off other women.

Often when women build up things in their heads, these imaginary episodes actually begin to occur. While she is trying to come up with some type of plan to ensure she is always number one in his life, she is neglecting what is most important, *her man!* When she thinks she has come up with the ultimate plan she has already lost the battle. It's all so perfect, what could have ever spoiled the plan? The answer is simple: *She* spoiled the plan. The neat and pretty picture she has drawn up in her head is soon to backfire. After a woman makes phone calls to his friends or family, her perfect image explodes. Since we already know women and men think differently, it is important to think with the head rather than the heart.

Men tend to have a negative outlook on life from the beginning. They are taught to be strong and learn how to support a family. So what happens when they need support? If they have a woman in their life at that time she is the person expected to give support. Once a woman has given a man this type of care, she feels everything is stable. At that point the relationship is actually at its shakiest. The woman is feeling very good about what she has done and wants more than anything to keep herself feeling this way. Her next action is to keep trying to force all of the emotion out of her man. Any type of aggressive behavior will make her man despise everything she had done. When a man shows affection, he doesn't expect to be turned down or feel any type of rejection.

Seeing a man's emotions, a woman feels that she has conquered all of the obstacles of this man. What she has done is put a huge responsibility upon herself. Not only does she have to worry about what she says, but she has to worry about all of her actions. Once a man realizes that he has given a part of his heart to a woman, he will pull back further and further until he feels safe again. What women shouldn't do is make a man disclose more information than he is really ready to.

Men do not like women who try to control everything. They like someone who has her own opinions and is capable of making intelligent decisions. When it comes to being aggressive, it should only go so far. It is great for a woman to know what she wants, but she should realize there are limitations. When you try to go that extra mile, it can create a problem that may be larger than you think. When women lie and cheat, they expand the gap by trying to get closer to their man. The next logical idea is to mend this gap.

There are never any easy roads to take in life because they all have twists and turns. To eliminate all of the unnecessary turbulence in your life as a woman, you need to think with your head instead of your heart. When you allow yourself to be open in front of others, you are giving them an opportunity to abuse you verbally, mentally, and physically. No one in the world wants to be hurt, but when you are, you become a stronger person.

Only time can heal wounds and only you can change the direction of the road you choose to take. Although some roads may be bumpier than others, these are the ones that end up being the most beneficial. When you have traveled on these roads you know what it is that should and should not be done.

It does not pay to be manipulative to get what you want. Once you have, it will no longer be something that you desire. To treat others with respect is to gain the greatest gift in life.

In order to love someone else you first have to love yourself. In any partnership, that may mean you have to swallow your pride sometimes and let the other person be right. Since most individuals are insecure about being alone, they need to treat their significant other as a special person instead of playing games all the time. Every game will come to an end and you best believe this is not one in which you will have a successful triumph. In this battle the only way to win is by being true and loving to who you are and who you are with.

There is a very thin line between love and hate, and when you walk on that line you are liable to slip a few times. But you have to get yourself back up and alter those behaviors that made you slip. If you keep your mind focused on the subject at hand, you will have no problem accomplishing your goal. Although not all women are the same and not all men are, we all have similar characteristics.

A dictionary definition of a sin is "an offensive weakened state of human nature." Going by this definition, when you lie you are just being weak. No man or woman in this world wants a weak companion by his or her side. In order to make it through any relationship you need to stay strong, which means not being in any kind of weakened state of mind.

Many women in this world feel that by keeping things hidden they will be able to live with themselves. What they don't realize is they can live *with* themselves but not *by* themselves.

When you take the spine out of a man's back, like my ex-wife did, sorry is not enough. What is amazing is when some people get a second chance to prove themselves, they do the same things over again.

In life there are actions that do involve life-long consequences; ruthless ambition leads to its own destruction. Relationships are what we need every day of our lives to stay sane and happy. Once we have found that significant other our lives have a lot more meaning. Try to keep your partner happy and content so you won't fall into the trap.

The only way to conquer relationships is by trying to make things as easy as possible. They can be very rewarding if you can see a good thing before it disappears. Since real-life situations induce motivation, I hope my experience can enlighten you on how to make your kinships work. No matter how much knowledge you acquire about the opposite gender, you will never fully understand their oppositional behaviors. Therefore, by working together through communication, relationships will become more united. Be open-minded, dig deep within, and use each experience as a way to build character.

Always being told that I would be a good football player, I got to experience the dream for two days during the "EdgeSports Shaving Gel" commercial.

CHAPTER 11

Character-Building Times

"We grow through our dreams. All great men and women are dreamers. Some, however, allow their dreams to die. You should nurse your dreams and protect them through bad times to the sunshine and light which always come."

—Woodrow Wilson

The challenges I faced for 13 years of my life in the DCFS system corrupted what was supposed to be a normal childhood. Every day I was locked up in the homes I felt exiled from the "real world." Not only was I isolated from my family, but all the friends I made eventually disappeared into thin air. I was moved around so many times my mind was discombobulated. Many times I would sit for hours, my mind blank. "If your mind were to go blank, how would you know?" (Ed Foreman).

In my jolted childhood I was faced with many developmental dilemmas. Each year I was faced with a different challenge, one more trying than the next. The biggest hurdle I had to face was trying to become a part of the mainstream school system.

When I entered as a high school freshman at Kenwood Academy, the feats I accomplished were unimaginable. Breaking track records, proving to the system that they were wrong, and making "real" friends helped to give me a stronger base.

If and when I see R. Kelly I'm going to thank him for all the times he didn't let the gangs mess with me, all the times I was short of money and he bought me food, and for believing in me when no one else did. As you know, he has gone on to be the king of rhythm and blues and one of the biggest names in the music industry. I have gone on to be the *Never Anything Too Easy* man, and we are both from the same school. He had his struggles coming up in the music business and I had my troubles coming up period.

After I made it through high school and met Nicosia, I believed I was set for life. There was no breaking the chains, or so I thought. Our children became the driving force behind my every move. It was easier to go through life knowing I had a purpose. I was going to be there for my children no matter who or what got in my way. I was determined to make it to the top and under no circumstances was I going to quit. When I heard "Daddy" come out of the mouths of my children, I was instantly stimulated. I put everything I had into making sure the Henry kids would have everything. The only thing that kept me alive were my five wonders in this world.

While I was playing basketball at Northeastern and in front of scouts, I began to realize my athletic abilities were not my most important gift. Writing a book was just a glimmer of a thought at first. I started thinking about all of the obstacles I had been through, which made me think that my experiences could help somebody else. Knowing that "80 percent of the people in the world don't care about your story, and the other 20 percent of them are just glad it wasn't them" (Les Brown), I still needed to get the story out because the world we live in needs help.

Many times you hear people with lots of questions and no answers. I'm here to answer many of them and add solutions. I have been through so much—being locked up, married, divorced, a part of DCFS, having a lot of children, being a basketball player, a student, working two jobs at once, and having a death in the family. I wanted to help others in the struggle to get over those situations. If this book can change one person's life, I have done my job.

You can get all the counseling in the world, but if that therapist or psychologist has never been through anything themselves, he or she can't always help. People want someone they can relate to. Real-life situations induce motivation. Going through all that I've been through makes people more comfortable opening up to me rather than someone who hasn't been through anything.

Instead of walking with your head down, keep it held high so all you can see is the sky. "We all know sometimes life's pain and sorrows can make you wish you were born in another time and space" (Stevie Wonder). But stay focused. Throughout the years of childhood traumas to adult misconceptions, I didn't allow family separation and bad experiences to keep me down. I chose not to focus on what happened in the past, but kept my head held high and went forward, knowing I was another day removed from the past, and another day closer to the future. I look at my past as character-building times. "If you don't act on life, life will act on you" (Les Brown).

When people ask you why you are always smiling, tell them it is because your mind doesn't register negative thoughts. People can't bring me out of my character or steal my joy. You know there are going to be people putting you down saying what you can't do. You will begin to even question yourself. I guarantee if you keep going with your idea it will happen for you. We are all extraordinary people capable of great things, but become phenomenal with God in our lives.

It's Not Over Until I Win

If current results are different
   Than what I thought when I began,
I must not quit and keep repeating:
   "It's not over until I win."
When doubters are all about me
   And I don't seem to have a friend,
I must say to myself once more,
   "It's not over until I win.
It's not over, no-not over,
   I must know this deep within.
In my mind, heart and spirit,
   It's not over until I win.
I will never give up!
   I won't ever give in!
I must never give out!
   No, it's not over until I win!
I affirm it every morning
   Through good and bad and thick and thin.
Every day I say with conviction…
   "It's not over until I win!"

—Les Brown and Celeste Johnson

In order to continue on with your positive
journey through life you have to live
   in the here and now.
The greatest tragedy in life is not death,
but life without a reason.
   It is dangerous to be alive and not know
   why you were given life.
The deepest craving of the human spirit is
to find a sense of significance and relevance.
The search for relevance in life is
   the ultimate pursuit of man.

—Myles Munroe

Throughout my journey many people helped me get through the difficult times. To my sisters Niece and Lennette and brother Keefe—we had a difficult life when Mama died, but I want to tell you I love you all very much. Each one of you is special. Promise me we will never change the tight sibling relationship we have. I hope my children are as close as we are. Corey "Hit Man" Hoger, Johnny Westmoreland, and Dorian Welch, thanks for being there for me during those hard times in my marriage. I don't know what road I would've gone down or how many "bids" (locked up in jail or incarcerated mentally) I would have done without you guys.

Women need to look within themselves to recognize what it is they really want. When you answer that question, implement your decision. Love, support, and cherish your man like your ancestors did. To all men of today, you have got to stay strong for the women of tomorrow. More important, take care of your children. Be there for your kids. Whatever it takes to revitalize your relationship with your children, do it! Think about this poem when you are down:

Advice to Men

No man knoweth love or hatred by
   all that is before them.
Do not pray for easy lives,
   Pray to be stronger men!
Do not pray for tasks equal to your powers.
   Pray for powers equal to your tasks.
For He shall bring every work into judgment.
   Be Thankful!

—Den of Thebes, Napata Assyeria

Knowing that life isn't simple for anyone, the more adversity I go through, the more I recognize I have to live for myself. Since my whole life has been ever changing against society, I have found no reason to try to conform to society's norms. Society does not define me. I am the only person who can validate who I am.

Having the ideal family is the American dream. When many of us think of the ideal family, we think of Mom, Dad, and children all living together in a nice house with a good life. The reality of that concept is that many times things do not work out that way.

Prayer of Serenity

God grant me the serenity
To accept the things I cannot change,
Courage to change the things I can,
And the wisdom to know the difference.

What people want and what they actually end up having depends on how their life began.

Many children start out under unfortunate conditions and end up going to foster care, group homes, and other family interventions. These children are affected mentally and physically. They need to know that with or without someone in their corner, they can succeed. Success is attainable no matter what; there is something out there for everyone. Surviving the odds is a part of life and I thank God for blessing me with each new day.

All children deserve both or at least one parent to love and care for them. For all children in the DCFS system, the only thing they can truly count on is God. The only way to become successful coming out of the DCFS system is to survive it. Every child in foster care should keep the faith in God and set their goals high. To every person who has gone through the *Never Anything Too Easy* experience, don't lose your focus.

Many people react on impulse and we must *learn* how to resist those impulses that may affect the rest of our lives. For example, don't let a little cigarette control your big body, or anything else for that matter. Maintain through each day, stay positive, disassociate yourself from negative people, think before you react, and remember as long as there's life there's hope! Be a *leader*. If you follow the crowd, you will get no further than the crowd. When people doubt you and don't think you can make it, don't give up. It's necessary to keep going. You must believe in yourself when no one else will. Then exercise the ultimate execution—massive success!!!

"Never Anything Too Easy," my life story straight to the top, not focusing on the past, but aiming for the future.

The Execution Is Massive Success

With a loaded gun to your head it seems as though you don't have many choices. One wrong move and BANG! That's what I felt every time I tried to better myself. With every movement I felt as though I could pull the trigger at any second. Instead of cocking the gun, I put it down and walked away. The first step was to make it out the door.

Basketball was my ticket to the stage. God had blessed me with a talent and I tried to utilize it to the fullest. Playing in the IIT Pro-Am tournament in Chicago, I was noticed by many different people. I used this acknowledgment as a tool to raise my self-esteem. I began to play better and look and feel better about everything.

Because I was close to Arthur Agee, I was able to meet the man with whom Arthur entrusted his story: Keith Kreiter. The internationally acclaimed documentary *Hoop Dreams* features Arthur and the story of his life. Arthur saw another story in *Never Anything Too Easy* and referred me to his agent. Other agents wouldn't give me a chance, but when I told Keith what I wanted to do he couldn't wait to become involved.

Keith called different publishing companies and a variety of "big" people to collaborate on the idea. I was overwhelmed with the initiative that Keith had taken on the project. It was as if Keith believed in the story almost as much as I did. With the image that I have, he was able to set up a couple of commercial shoots for me. The idea was that if I was on national television, with my already known name of Baby Kemp, this new found fame would expedite the project!

Low and behold he did just that. I received a call early one morning from Keith saying that there was a commercial being taped with Brett Favre and Reggie White from the Green Bay Packers. I went to the audition and to my surprise, I made the final cut. I was chosen for a small part in a national Edge Gel shaving cream commercial. It played a substantial part in my upcoming debut. Being able to mingle with the best of them, I learned the most vital part of networking—word of mouth.

I met Joe Sweeney, Brett Favre's marketing agent, who was overwhelmed by my powerful story. Throughout the two days I participated in the commercial I had the opportunity to talk to different people about my story. Even commercial and movie producer Stan Schofield couldn't comprehend how such a young man had gone through all of these trials and tribulations and was still standing.

My connection with Stan helped to enhance my dream of making a movie. He gave me hope that my story was unique and powerful. As we discussed the endless possibilities for my story, we formed a common ground. "Once a man or a woman's mind is expanded with an idea or concept, it can never be satisfied going back to where it was" (Les Brown).

With all of this positive encouragement there was no way I was going to stop. I wanted my face to be seen on every possible media force. God must have heard my prayer, because I got another call from Keith Kreiter. This time he presented me with an audition for a basketball player. Those who made the cut would be in a national McDonald's commercial with Grant Hill and Larry Bird. This was right up my alley. Not only was I able

102

to show my skills, but I was going to meet the legendary Larry Bird.

With these commercials under my belt I started to explore my other options.

The Road Not Taken

Two roads diverged in a yellow wood,
And sorry I could not travel both
And be one traveler, long I stood
And looked down one as far as I could
To where it bent in the undergrowth;

Then took the other, as just as fair,
And having perhaps the better claim,
Because it was grassy and wanted wear;
Though as for that the passing there
Had worn them really about the same,

And both that morning equally lay
In leaves no step had trodden black.
Oh, I kept the first for another day!
Yet knowing how way leads on to way,
I doubted if I should ever come back.

I shall be telling this with a sigh
Somewhere ages and ages hence:
Two roads diverged in a wood, and I—

I took the one less traveled by,
And that has made all the difference.

—Robert Frost

As you may have guessed, I took the road less traveled. I began my path with a trip to the West Side of Chicago. Although I grew up there, visiting the area now made me see a different side of this impoverished place. Every Saturday for six weeks I attended the Les Brown workshop for up and coming motivational speakers. I was surrounded by positive people who all were determined to make it. In class we listened to Les talk and learned what was involved in becoming a motivational speaker.

After listening to Les's story I was able to relate to his experiences and learn from what he had done. Everyone was against him, but he found a way to overcome all of the opposition. I knew that if he did it, then I could do it. The phrases he uses, and the way I felt during the time I spent with him, were incredible. His response to my story influenced my determination to reach for the unthinkable. After completing these impacting weeks there was no doubt in my mind that I was going to get my master's degree. I put together a letter and sent it out to 10 different colleges.

As I was growing up, I went through many childhood traumas and experienced what it was like to be a part of the DCFS and foster homes system. I was separated from my family and all of the people I loved. All the kids around me seemed so different. There was every culture you could imagine all in one place. I knew all of the kids were not like me, but I learned we all could get along. The friendships we formed were the only way we could make it through the devastating reality of life.

Now that I've overcome the problems of my youth, I want to help other kids who have been dealt an unfortunate hand.

What I have learned through my experiences, I have been able to apply to my real-life situations.

As of the writing of this book, I am a childcare worker (CCW) at Lydia Children's Home in Chicago. This institution has given me another chance to experience what it is like to have many cultures come together. Here the multicultural staff works together for one common goal, which is the best possible life for the children. It constantly reminds me of what I used to go through and has inspired me to acquire my MSW in social work.

Lydia is a residential home located in Chicago for children who do not live with their parents for one reason or another. Lydia focuses on having the children lead a normal life and help them so they will be able to reach their ultimate goals. At Lydia the children are taught basic living skills, oppositional behaviors, social skills, and ways to interact with all cultures and ethnicities. The positive focus of Lydia has kept them in business for more than 80 years. Since they focus on the positive, I am a perfect addition to their staff.

As CCW, I have many different responsibilities. The most important is giving children the love and support they need to make it through life. Every day I work with the children on life situations. I use extra curricular activities to demonstrate how frustration can be eliminated. Like my friends Eddie Wardlaw and John Stewart play basketball as a tool to let out aggression, I wanted my boys to do the same.

By helping these children I feel as though I am giving back to the system. I know how it felt to be confined, alone, and desperate for attention. I was determined to make sure the children at Lydia would not have these types of feelings. They all are special with dreams and aspirations and with my assistance they are going to attain their objectives.

I work with children here to come up with the best possible strategies to solve their own issues. I try to help alter the child's negative actions. I do this by encouraging the child to be self-motivated. They receive pats on the back, high fives, and smiles as their main source of gratification.

My double bachelor's degrees in psychology and speech performing arts/communications have given me a basis to work with children, but I yearn for more effective ways to enhance my knowledge. I hope to learn the best and most effective ways in which to help children and their families gain more positive reinforcement. I know that education will assist me in reaching my future career goals.

After completing my MSW in social work I am going to take what I have learned and use it to comfort and help my family, as well as those who have experienced turbulence in their lives. My biggest sense of accomplishment has been to help my children and the children I work with reach their ultimate goals. Someday I plan to open up my own Never Anything Too Easy Youth Centers. I hope to have a home that will be a melting pot for all different cultures. I want all of the children and staff to feel that they can learn from one another. I know from experience that growing up around many cultures helps a person become less racist and more versatile.

As I am pursuing my master's degree, I will continue to work with Lydia. I know that I will benefit from your teachings in the Master's program of Social Work, as will all of the children and families with whom I come in contact. Families are a child's main source of connection and my desire is to make this an unbreakable bond.

The key to a successful future is to have a genuine goal that cannot be taken away by anyone. When I finally got out of the system after 13 years my goal was to give back to them in any way possible. The positive path was to get into the system to find a way to help others. I thank Beverly Humphries for giving me the opportunity to show my endearment toward the kids. It took someone like her to interview me and know that I was the right candidate to fulfill the position. She is so unique and professional. Beverly consistently performs many tasks at the same time she focuses on the children. She is truly a scholar and one of a kind.

The execution is massive success and I was not going to do it any other way. When I open up the Never Anything Too Easy Youth Centers, it will be a facility filled with positive and energetic people. Everybody should want to make a difference beyond themselves. "Don't be bitter, be better. Don't waste that energy being bitter" (G. Piere). Your elders before you have made a path; so use it, don't abuse it! Younger generations, don't rebel so much against the old; open your mind to learning from their experience. In showing your maturity be patient, often too many times everyone wants to go to the party, but nobody wants to stay and clean up. I know sometimes it doesn't seem like they care but they do. Ask for help, not because you're weak, but because you want to remain strong.

I think of myself as the comeback kid. After all, life is 10 percent of what happens to you and 90 percent of how you react to it. I now have taken what I have learned to add to my motivational speaking skills. "If you are not on your way to being your best, then you are in the way of your own progress" (Gwenn Pierre).

Besides motivational speaking I look to attain my PhD in world relations. I have arrived at the completion of Maslow's hierarchy of needs. My self-fulfilling prophecy has been to give promise to others in desperation. This material will help to medicate the minds of the whole population. Satisfaction comes from modification of surging through the world's problems. Remember the 5 "P"s—Proper Preparation Prevents Poor Performance!

To color your day so that the outlook is positive throughout, and your will and drive are increased, affirm this to yourself:

If you want a thing bad enough to go out and
fight for it, to work day and night for it,
to give up your time, your peace and
your sleep for it . . .
if all that you dream and scheme is about it,

*and life seems useless and worthless
    without it...*
*if you gladly sweat for it and fret for it
    and plan for it and lose all your terror
    of the opposition for it . . .*
*if you simply go after that thing you want
    with all of your capacity, strength and
    sagacity, faith, hope and confidence
    and stern pertinacity...*
*if neither cold, poverty, famine, nor gout,
    sickness nor pain, of body and brain,
    can keep you away from that thing
    you want...*
*if dogged and grim you beseech and
    beset it, with the help of God,
    you WILL get it!*

—Berton Braley

The ultimate revenge is to retaliate with massive success.

Antonia Krystle Henry, Trinidad and Tobago Supermodel . . . taking the world by storm!

Kahlilah Inez Henry, the world's next Sparkling Movie Star from Trinidad and Tobago.

NEVER
ANYTHING
TOO
EASY:
The Movement

(top) Here's Trinidad's very own Kalilah and Antonia Henry with their billion dollar smiles, posing for their future Disney TV sitcom.

(upper right) Daddy Christmas shopping with Antonia and Kalilah.

(bottom right) Here's Kalilah Inez Henry thinking about opening a chain of Trinidadian restaurants in her country.

110